COLL AND TIREE

THEIR PREHISTORIC FORTS
AND ECCLESIASTICAL ANTIQUITIES

WITH NOTICES OF ANCIENT REMAINS IN
THE TRESHNISH ISLES

BY

ERSKINE BEVERIDGE

AUTHOR OF

'THE CHURCHYARD MEMORIALS OF CRAIL' ETC.

WITH SEVENTY-SEVEN FULL-PAGE ILLUSTRATIONS
AND TWO MAPS

ORIGIN

*The Publisher would like to thank Mairi Hedderwick
for making this publication possible.*

This facsimile edition published in 2018 by
Origin, an imprint of
Birlinn Limited
West Newington House
10 Newington Road
Edinburgh EH9 1QS

www.birlinn.co.uk

First published in 1903 by Edinburgh University Press

ISBN 978 1 91247 603 9
eBook ISBN 978 1 788851 10 7

British Library Cataloguing-in-Publication Data
A catalogue record for this book is available from
the British Library

Printed and bound in Great Britain by Clays Ltd, Elcograf S.p.A.

PREFACE

THE primary object of this volume is to describe the Prehistoric Duns or Forts of Coll and Tiree, from observations made upon successive visits to these islands during the summers of 1896 to 1901.

This undertaking has been found specially interesting, and at the same time the more difficult, because of its dealing with an almost virgin soil. The only authoritative work upon our Scottish Duns is Dr. Christison's *Early Fortifications in Scotland*,[1] which, in the descriptive text, does not include any one of the sites now under consideration, although the Table entitled 'Dun in Scottish Place-names' enumerates fifteen of them, and the appended Bibliographical List gives references to papers read before the Society of Antiquaries of Scotland, in which incidental notice is taken of two of the Duns in Coll and of other two in Tiree.

In his self-imposed task, the writer has found no printed topographical matter so helpful as a paper by Captain F. W. L. Thomas *On the Duns of the Outer Hebrides* (in *Archæologia Scotica*, vol. v. part iii., Edin. 1890), whilst this aid was merely collateral, its subject (as the title implies) being strictly confined to the 'Long Island' from Barra to Lewis.

[1] Edin., 1898—*The Rhind Lectures in Archæology for* 1894.

As to oral assistance, grateful acknowledgment is made to Dr. Joseph Anderson, for advice and hints, with the further favour of his consent to read the following pages before they were put to press. Part of that advice was to simply describe what was seen, and to leave inferences alone. This was found to be a very hard saying, and yet an honest endeavour has been made to adopt it, so far as was found possible. The same recommendation has since appeared in print from another source : 'The best thing to do is simply to describe the objects and place of finding, and let philosophers see to the dates.' This is undoubtedly a counsel of perfection, but such counsels are proverbially difficult to put into practice.

The study, from a 'comparative' view, of Prehistoric forts in general, has received due attention, as will probably be admitted upon the ground of special visits made to most of the Outer Hebrides—including North and South Uist, Harris and Lewis,—as also to Jura, Colonsay, Knapdale, Glenelg, Caithness, and Sutherland, in addition to a somewhat laborious drive in Irish cars round the coast of Donegal.

One of the greatest difficulties experienced has been to avoid making too much of some of the badly preserved sites, especially in the island of Coll, and simply to describe them as accurately as possible, without lending undue prominence either to any distinctive feature or theory.

At most, only nine Duns in Coll and three in Tiree, out of

sixty-one in all (excluding the Treshnish Isles), are to be classed in the really 'unsatisfactory' category—by no means a large proportion; while, of those twelve, two are so included because it was not found practicable to examine them personally, other two bear the traditional name of 'Dun,' and still another pair are locally known as 'Carn' and 'Carnan.'

In Scotland the descriptive term 'Dun' appears to be simply the Gaelic for 'a heap, a hill,' and hence appropriated to the forts, which were almost invariably situated upon an elevation, either natural or artificial. It is curious to notice that the word 'Broch' (derived from the Anglo-Saxon 'burh' or Norse 'borg'), has experienced an almost diametrically opposite transition—first signifying 'a fortified place,' and latterly applied to a town—our 'burgh'—evidently because these were originally placed within fortifications.

The true Brochs (as is elsewhere stated) have been assigned to a period roughly defined as lying between the Roman invasion of Scotland, in the first century A.D., and the cessation of the incursions of the Scandinavian Vikings after the eleventh century. The chronology of the Duns is more complicated, and, as regards the Hebrides, the only tenable conclusion appears to be that while they are prehistoric in origin, the period of their erection cannot be placed later than the ninth to the thirteenth century, some of them probably dating back even so far as the Christian era—or beyond it. The true Brochs (of Glenelg, Lewis, Caithness,

Orkney, etc.) seem certainly to have been found standing by the Vikings when they invaded our shores in the ninth century. And, as regards the simpler Duns, it is significant that the Norsemen of that period were not accustomed to stone-building in their native Scandinavia. There are indeed in Norway the remains of rude stone forts upon hill-tops and other strong natural positions, but we are unaware that any distinctive period is assigned to them. The *Proc. Soc. Antiq. Scot.* (vol. xii. p. 321) quotes the consensus of opinion among Norwegian archæologists (regarding their own country) to the following effect: 'As long as Paganism reigned throughout the land, all buildings were constructed of timber. On the introduction of Christianity (that is, in the beginning of the eleventh century) our forefathers first learned to employ lime and stone in building; but as the art followed in the train of the new doctrine, it was for a long time only employed in the service of the spiritual power, and used alone in the construction of churches, monastic buildings, and bishops' palaces.' It will be seen that this account takes no notice of the Norwegian 'Borgs' or 'Bygdeborge' which were built without lime, and irregular in form.

As regards Iceland, the Sagas make occasional references to 'strengths' or 'borgs'; but these seem chiefly to have been of turf and wood. A single exception (and very noteworthy in its resemblance to a good specimen of the Hebridean Dun) still exists at Borgarvirki in west Iceland, and is figured in *A Pilgrimage to*

the Saga-Steads of Iceland. This is ascribed (with some probability) to Bardi, of the 'Heath-Slayings,' and is therefore
considered as dating from early in the eleventh century, not
later indeed than A.D. 1021.

Whether or not Bardi had visited our Hebrides, and thence
copied this solitary known stone-Fort in Iceland, history and
tradition are alike silent. In point of fact he was lineally
descended from Ketil Flatnef 'of the Sudreys,' his mother
(Thurida) being a daughter of Olaf the Peacock, who again was
great-grandson of Thorstein the Red, a grandson of Ketil, the
earliest of all Vikings to appear by name in the Hebrides. Olaf
the Peacock is recorded to have visited Ireland,[1] and his sister
Hallgerda had been fostered by Thiostolf, 'a Southislander by
stock' (or man of the Sudreys).[2] These circumstances are quite
inconclusive, although they point to the likelihood of Bardi's
having taken part in the Viking raids upon the Hebrides, which
indeed were carried on with special vigour by (King) Olaf
Tryggwason between about the years A.D. 990-1000.

---

[1] Olaf the Peacock presented to his cousin Gunnar 'a cloak which Moorkjartan the Erse
King owned' and a hound which had been given him in Ireland. This was in A.D. 988,
according to Dasent's *Burnt Njal*, vol. i. pp. ccii, 192, 223. It is barely possible that
Borgarvirki (of probable date *ca.* 1013-1021), and even the Norwegian Stone-Forts, may
have been erected after the model of Duns in our own islands. There are two alterna-
tives—either that the case was *vice versâ*, which would hardly give a sufficiently early date
for the Scottish Forts, or that both the Norwegian and Scottish Duns are copies or evolu-
tions from a still more primary type, and that of eastern origin. This latter, to our mind,
would thoroughly fulfil all the conditions.

[2] *Ibid.*, vol. i. p. 30.

To come to more recent times, it seems certain that some of the ancient forts of Coll and Tiree were utilised, if only as occasional refuges, within the distinctly historic period. In North Uist are several Duns of more elaborate type, which appear to have been built in even mediæval times; and it is there—upon an island in Loch Caravat—that the writer found the solitary specimen, out of more than a hundred examined in the Western Isles, in which mortar has been used in the original construction.

In a few examples the names of forts in Coll and Tiree occur as bi-lingual pleonasms—both the Celtic and the Norse being represented in the same title—as Dun Boraige Mor and Dun Boraige Beg in Tiree, and Dun Borbaidh (pronounced *Borive*) in Coll; while, outside the scope of the present volume, Dun Borve appears at least three times in the nomenclature of Hebridean forts, twice in Skye and once in Lewis.

The word 'Dun' is widely spread throughout the topography of north-west Europe, and a reduplicated form seems even to exist in Le-Bourg-Dun (a hamlet near Dieppe) and Dunaburg (Russia), although in each instance there is closely associated a stream or river bearing part of the name—the *Dun* and the *Dvina* respectively, whatever may be their derivation.[1]

The ancient Earth-Dwelling or 'Erd-House,'—often found in

[1] Mr. Thomas J. Westropp in his exhaustive monograph upon *The Ancient Forts of Ireland (Trans. Royal Irish Academy,* 1902) gives, for comparison, ground-plans of Hill-Forts of somewhat similar type in Cornwall, Wales, France, Sweden, Russia, Bohemia, Hungary, Bosnia, and Thessaly; as also of Lake-Forts in Holland and Prussia.

the Hebrides, although only one is known in the islands under consideration—would also seem to have had widely extended use. A recent visitor to Ungava Bay, Labrador, describes the Eskimo dwellings as of three kinds, the third, or *Igloshuak*, being 'simply an underground cellar or tilt. It is impossible to stand upright in such a residence, but the natives being small in stature experience no difficulty on this point. A subterranean passage about twelve feet long forms the principal entrance to the house, and it requires no small amount of gymnastic agility to wend one's way through. A square hole in the roof serves a like purpose.' This *Igloshuak* appears strongly to resemble an Earth-House, both in size and arrangement.

In regard to patterned pottery a far-away analogy may also be cited. In *A Mound of Many Cities; or Tell el Hesy Excavated*, by Fred. J. Bliss, Ph.D. (2nd ed. 1898, *Palestine Exploration Fund*) are figured sixty-seven fragments of pottery bearing simple marks, many of them practically identical with those to be found in the Duns or upon the Sandhills of Coll and Tiree. To these is deliberately assigned (*Ibid.*, p. 43) a date of *ca.* 1600 B.C., reaching back to the Amorite or Pre-Israelitish occupation of the Land of Canaan. It may be taken as axiomatic that such primitive types would persist throughout many successive ages, so that the above is quoted, not as an argument upon chronology, but simply to prove that time and space made little difference in the rude designs on pottery.

Upon the subject of Sandhill sites, a fact which presents a strong contrast to those last adduced may here be mentioned. It is well known that the Culbin sands (near the mouth of the river Findhorn, Morayshire) have been found rich in flint arrow-heads, scrapers, and articles of bronze (but many of the latter, strictly speaking, of *brass*). These flints testify to a very early occupation, but the specimens in brass and iron apparently belong to a comparatively modern period, so late as from the thirteenth to the seventeenth centuries, the tract in question having been probably occupied until its complete devastation by blown sand about the year 1695 (*Proc. Soc. Antiq. Scot.*, vol. xii. p. 305).

One fact (which, to be sure, cuts both ways) must be admitted, that upon revisiting known sites during a series of years, both as regards Duns and Sandhills (which latter vary in conformation with every wind that blows), some fresh information has almost invariably been gathered.

Chapter III. (upon ancient Hut-Circles in Coll) is completely re-written upon very different lines from its first conception, and undoubtedly with a greater measure of correctness, although, even as it stands, perhaps only two, out of the five separate ruins mentioned, afford any serious basis for deduction.

In Chapter XVI., upon the Norwegian Occupation of the Hebrides, the aim has been to follow the safest chronology; first, the *Rolls* edition of the Sagas (when dates are there given), and secondly, other high authorities, as Anderson's *Orkneyinga Saga*,

Dasent's *Burnt Njal*, and Skene's *Celtic Scotland*. The dates noted from James Johnstone's *Antiquitates Celto-Scandicæ*, of 1786, almost certainly need revision, but failing this (and the higher the source, the less readily is a precise year affixed during such periods as the eighth to tenth centuries), no alternative has been found.

Munch's *The Chronicle of Man and the Sudreys*, a most valuable monograph, was printed in 1860, and where recent writers, as Vigfusson (*Rolls* edition of the Sagas) and Dasent, have differed upon chronology, we may believe that it has been with good reason.

Between the four authorities last mentioned, perhaps the widest divergence is in regard to the date of death of Thorstein the Red—some fourteen years; another *crux* has been the battle of Hafursfjord, usually assigned to A.D. 872, but here Skene (*Celtic Scotland*) has been followed with the year A.D. 883, upon what appear to be good grounds, although unfortunately, in stating these, that author has not specifically given his references.

Dr. Johnson and his faithful henchman, Boswell, became involuntary visitors to the island of Coll during the late autumn of 1773, and were there storm-stayed for ten days. Sailing from Skye, they had reached Loch Eatharna (the bay at Arinagour) on the evening of Sunday, 3rd October, and for a week were entertained in the modern house of Breacacha by the (younger)

Laird of Coll. Other two nights were evidently spent at Achamore and Grishipol, and those of arrival and the eve of departure (*i.e.* the 3rd and 13th October) at anchor in sloops off Arinagour.

Dr. Johnson's own account affords very much less of topographical or other detail than is to be found in Boswell's 'Journal,' which latter distinctly refers (without specifically naming them) to the Sandhills of Totronald and Traigh Foill, and to a lead-mine at Crossapol. Vestiges of old dwellings are described at Traigh Foill, the lower part of the walls then still standing above the drifted surface. As to these sandhills (but also indefatigably upon almost every occasion) Boswell—to our amusement, if not edification—in his usual naïve manner, records the great lexicographer's *obiter dicta*.

It is locally stated that Dr. Johnson visited Dun Acha, which indeed seems highly probable, although no reference is found, either in his own Journal or that of Boswell, to this or any other Dun in Coll.

In the following pages, several variations of orthography certainly occur; but the system has been adopted of spelling each word (so far as quotations are concerned) exactly according to the authority cited. The Gaelic language, however, has proved wholly unmanageable in regard to place-names. Some of these are no doubt given with strict accuracy, but more often the Ordnance Survey Map has been followed, or in the case of familiar names (such, for instance, as *Arinagour* and *Acha*), the phonetic or anglicised form is adopted.   In any event, it affords some consolation to recognise that the Gaelic language is indeterminate, varying in different localities and also according to the expert consulted.

In conclusion, hearty acknowledgment is made of invaluable assistance rendered by Mr. Angus MacIntyre (now United Free Church Missionary at Lochmaddy, but formerly stationed in Coll), with whom the writer has visited almost all the sites here described in the island of Coll, in addition to many others (for the sake of comparison) in both North and South Uist.

This volume is now submitted as the result of six years' investigation of its subject, and in the hope that it will be found to contain as few inaccuracies as may be compatible with the difficult and often intricate nature of the undertaking.

ERSKINE BEVERIDGE.

St. Leonard's Hill,
Dunfermline.

CONTRACTIONS USED IN REFERRING TO AUTHORITIES UPON EARLY HEBRIDEAN HISTORY AND THE NORSE SAGAS, ESPECIALLY IN CHAPTERS XIV—XVI.

Burnt Njal. 'The Story of Burnt Njal; or, Life in Iceland at the end of the Tenth Century.' From the Icelandic of the Njals Saga, by (Sir) G. W. Dasent. 2 vols. Edin., 1861.

Celtic Scotland. 'Celtic Scotland: a History of Ancient Alban.' By William F. Skene, D.C.L., LL.D. Reference is throughout made to the second edition. 3 vols. Edin., 1886-1890.

Celto-Norman. 'Antiquitates Celto-Normannicæ; containing the Chronicle of Man and the Isles.' Edited by James Johnstone. Copenhagen, 1786.

Celto-Scand. 'Antiquitates Celto-Scandicæ; etc.' Edited from various Sagas by James Johnstone. Copenhagen, 1786.

Collectanea. 'Collectanea de Rebus Albanicis, etc.' Edited by the Iona Club. Edin., 1847.

Fowler's *Adamnan.* 'Adamnani Vita S. Columbæ.' Edited from Dr. Reeves' text, by J. T. Fowler, M.A., D.C.L. Oxford, 1894.

Henderson's *Iceland.* 'Iceland; or the Journal of a Residence in that Island during the years 1814 and 1815.' By the Rev. Ebenezer Henderson, D.D. 2 vols. Edin., 1818.

Keary. 'The Vikings in Western Christendom, A.D. 789 to A.D. 888.' By C. F. Keary. London, 1891.

Munch. 'The Chronicle of Man and the Sudreys.' Edited by Professor P. A. Munch. Christiania, 1860.

Orkneyinga Saga. 'The Orkneyinga Saga.' Edited by Joseph Anderson, LL.D. Edin., 1873.

Reeves' *Adamnan.* 'The Life of St. Columba, founder of Hy; written by Adamnan.' By William Reeves, D.D. Dublin, 1857.

Reeves' *Monograph.* 'The Island of Tiree.' By William Reeves, D.D., in 'The Ulster Journal of Archæology,' No. 8, October 1854, pp. 233-244.

Rolls, or *Rolls* edition of the Sagas. 'Icelandic Sagas and other Historical Documents relating to the Settlements and Descents of the Northmen on the British Isles.' Edited by G. Vigfusson (vols. i. and ii.), and by Sir G. W. Dasent (vol. iii.). Published under the direction of the Master of the Rolls. 3 vols. London, 1887-1894.

Saga Library. 'The Saga Library.' Edited by William Morris and Eirikr Magnusson. 5 vols. London, 1891-1895.

TABLE OF CONTENTS

CHAPTER XIV.

CHAPTER XV.

CHAPTER XVI.

LIST OF ILLUSTRATIONS

MAPS.

FULL-PAGE PLATES.

COLL AND TIREE

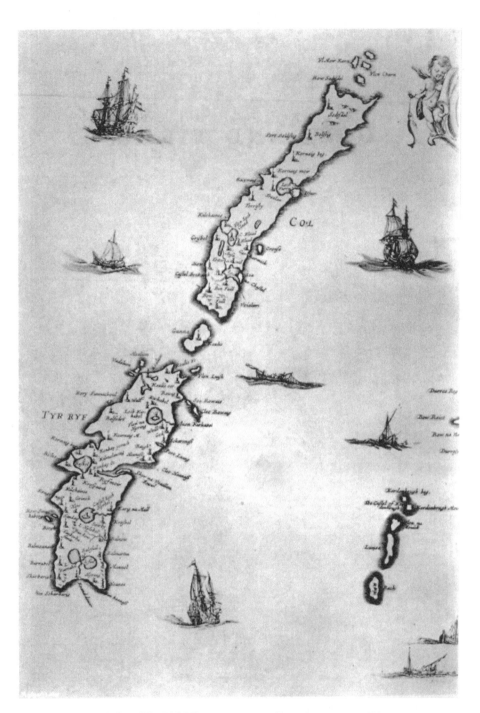

COLL AND TIREE, REDUCED FROM BLAEU'S ATLAS OF 1662.

CHAPTER I

COLL—GENERAL

THE Island of Coll, one of the Inner Hebrides, is situated seven miles west from the nearest point of Mull. Its trend is from the north-east to south-west, fully twelve miles in length, with an average breadth of about three miles. In surface Coll is most irregular, consisting chiefly of groups of small rocky hills covered with a scanty coating of soil. Ben Hogh, of 339 feet, near the middle of its western shore, is the highest elevation, while several others exceed 200 feet; fresh-water lochs are numerous, especially towards the north-east, but all are small, only three approaching half a mile in length.

The present population is sparse, not much exceeding 400, a condition almost to be expected from the small proportion of arable soil. Upon the other hand, judging from its many sites of ancient chapels, Coll must have been, by comparison, thickly peopled in pre-Reformation times.[1]

In treating of the ancient remains in Coll, mention may first be made of an underground gallery—apparently the only site, in either of the islands now under notice, which can be classed as an

[1] Sir John Sinclair's *Statistical Account* (first edn., 1794) quotes the population of Coll as 1193 in 1755, and 1041 in 1793. The latest census (of 1901) gives only 432, as against 522 in 1891.

'Earth-House' or subterranean dwelling. This structure is at ARINABOST[1] (two miles north-west from the small village of Arinagour[2]), only a few yards south from the point of junction of the roads thence running south-west and south-east. It was discovered upon the levelling of the west (or Ballyhogh) highway about the year 1855, when a piece of twisted gold was found, evidently part of a bracelet. The original entrance is believed to have been to the north of the road last mentioned, in a spot now covered by the dwelling (a former schoolhouse) which immediately adjoins. The passage still extends south-eastward in a flattened arc for 38 feet from beneath the porch of this house, under the road, and emerging into the remains of a roughly circular chamber 7 feet in diameter, now laid bare in a gravel pit. The greatest present interior height of the gallery is 50 inches, with a width of about 27 inches, and the walls are clearly mere underground linings ; the roof consists of broad stone lintels at short intervals, bound together by narrower transverse slabs, either at right angles or in pairs diagonally.[3] The chamber, disclosed in the gravel-pit at the south-east extremity, was partially

[1] Derived from the Gaelic *airidh na* (shieling of the), and the Norse *bolstadr* (homestead), being thus a hybrid place-name.

[2] 'Shieling of the goats,' the only village in Coll, and the port of the island.

[3] Part of the roof is stated to have been of wood, and the passage to have extended farther north than the porch of the old schoolhouse. 'Earth-Houses' occur over a wide area in Scotland, chiefly in the eastern counties, and sometimes in groups. They are rare towards the west coast and in the Hebrides, although the writer knows of several in North and South Uist. Their date is attributed to the period 'between the time of the general establishment of Christianity and the departure of the Romans from Scotland' (Anderson's *Scotland in Pagan Times : The Iron Age*, p. 304)—say A.D. 400-1000.

ARINAGOUR, FROM NORTH.

excavated in the summer of 1896 by Mr. Robert Sturgeon, post-master of Coll, who unearthed some quantity of kitchen-midden bones and shells, a large bronze pin with a fluted head, at least two fragments of flint, and a few bits of crude unglazed pottery. In the same place was found a large glass bead (cylindrical in shape and about half an inch long) of an indigo blue colour, and enamelled with white spiral ornament.

The ground to the south-east is low and flat, being even to this day sometimes styled *Loch* Arinabost, a name which it is said to have justified within living memory.

CHAPTER II

COLL—DUNS, OR ANCIENT FORTS

THE Duns of Coll are, almost without exception, either of the rude Hill-Fort type, occupying the irregular summits of rocks, sometimes rugged in the extreme, or of the artificial or semi-artificial Islet type, which is here well represented. The great majority are unmarked upon the six-inch Ordnance Survey map, the compilers of that most useful work having evidently paid far less attention to the ancient sites in Coll than to those in the sister island of Tiree.

In Coll the semi-Broch type—described under Class A in Tiree—seems to be unrepresented, unless indeed the Loch Dun in Poll nam Broig (*postea*, No. 21, BREACACHA), now completely defaced, may possibly have been of this character.

CLASS B

ROCK-FORTS, OR HILL-FORTS—usually close to the shore.

These have certainly been fortifications, the defences invariably taking the form of a strong exterior dry-stone rampart on the side of access, which was ordinarily at one point only, and boundary walls around the irregular summit of the rock itself. None of these walls now exceed 2 or 3 feet in height, and, so far as can be judged, they never were at all lofty. Inside are commonly to be traced the foundations of several separate dwellings, often circular in shape, and these, it may be conjectured, have consisted of but a few courses of stone—always uncemented—at the base, probably continued higher by turf, and roofed in with wood. In many instances the remains of other small buildings, evidently subsidiary and of the same period, occur outside the boundary walls, though nearly adjacent.

Commencing at the north-east end of Coll, and following the course of the sun, the Duns of this type are here enumerated.

Upon the east coast of the island, a mile south of Sorisdale,[1] and immediately to the south of Meall na h'Iolaire (259 feet) are the scanty ruins of DUN DULORICHAN.[2] This name was obtained •1 from local sources and does not appear upon the Ordnance map.[3]

The fort is 200 to 300 yards east from the small Loch Airidh Raonuill, and clearly within sight of the Island Dun in Loch Fada, three-quarters of a mile due west. The approach has been from the north, the rock being precipitous in the other directions, and here, well up the hillside, are distinct remains of a defensive wall. Upon the summit, in the interior of the Dun, are also the founda-

[1] This is the local pronunciation. Upon the present maps the spelling is 'Sodisdale,' and in Blaeu's Atlas of 1662 'Sotsdel,' both evidently identical with the 'Terra de Sotesdal' mentioned in a charter of Pope Innocent III., of date 9th Dec. 1203 (*Munch*, p. 152).

[2] Perhaps *Dun-orachain*, 'the fort of the jewel.' The marginal numbers, as •1, etc., +I, etc., correspond with the positions (of forts and chapels respectively) similarly marked in red upon the map of Coll and Tiree which is appended.

[3] The name, 'Tulbrichan (Danish Fort),' is here shown upon a large map of Scotland published by A. and C. Black, but this is probably due to a purely clerical error in transcribing from one authority to another.

tions of small isolated huts, while those of one or two others exist upon the lower ground to the north-east. Apart from these, no other sign was to be found of its former occupation.

Between Dulorichan and the next Hill-Fort to the south-west (as at present known to the writer) is a long distance—nearly five and a half miles as the crow flies.[1] This Fort is upon the summit of DRUIM AN AIRIDH FHADA, about 300 yards from the small Loch Boidheach, and nearly two miles south-west from Arinagour. Its position is practically in the centre of the island of Coll, of which, moreover, perhaps no other hill commands so complete a general view. Here are the remains of a most distinct circular mound, 20 yards across and some 10 feet in height, capped by an inner stone wall with a few large stones in its base, enclosing an area of about 15 yards in diameter, upon which lie many smaller stones. In the valley to the west are the two 'Mill' Lochs with their Island Duns to be noted later. This Dun is nearly two miles from the nearest shore, and is thus much more remote from the coast than any other Hill-Fort to be noticed in Coll.[2]

Next in order, about two miles to the south-west, comes

---

[1] In all probability a Dun exists (or existed) near Sorisdale at the extreme north-east of Coll. Others may perhaps be discovered upon the comparatively unexplored east coast of the island, between Dulorichan and Loch Eatharna. CNOC NA' DUIN (No. 17) at Arinagour is only four miles south-west from Dulorichan, but this site is so indistinct (as in the case of the neighbouring CARNAN, No. 18) that it cannot be definitely classified. Island Duns— Nos. 23, 25, 26, 27—do indeed occur within the wide intervening space between Nos. 1 and 2, but these, from their position in hollows, could not have carried on that visual connection through a chain of forts which is so unmistakably suggested upon the seaward side of Coll, and upon both sides of Tiree.

[2] The next in distance from the shore is Dun Acha (No. 3), while other three near Hogh and Gallanach (Nos. 8, 10, and 14) are about half a mile inland.

STONE IMPLEMENT OR WEAPON, DUN ACHA.

DUN ACHA, FROM NORTH.

DUN ACHA. This occupies the summit of an isolated ridge
—long and narrow—by the roadside a little south of Acha
Mill, and almost a mile from the shore. Acha (or 'field') is
evidently merely a place-name, and to follow local tradition, the
Dun ought to be known as 'Dun Bhorlum[1] mhic Anlaimh righ
Lochlinn,' meaning either 'The fort of the ridge of the son of
Olaf, King of Norway,' or, by possibility, 'The fort of Borlum,
son of,' etc.

The story runs that Dun Acha was the stronghold of a Norseman, the son of Anlaimh (or Olaf), and that the native islanders,
in despair under his tyranny, resolved to attack it in force upon
the first suitable opportunity. Accordingly they one night set
fire to the Dun, and thus succeeded in routing the foreigners.
This testimony of folklore seems to be borne out, as regards the
burning of the fort, by the numerous evidences of fire still visible
in its foundations—a fact specially noted by the writer long before
he heard the tradition.

Dun Acha is strongly situated, covering the centre of the
abrupt rock already described, at an elevation of about 150 feet
above the sea-level. The lower portions of its walls, though
showing no very large stones, are distinctly traceable at many
points, especially upon the north-west edge and across the
entrance at the north end. The gateway is 33 inches wide,
and leads to a small plateau, some 12 yards long, whence
the access to the main fort—another plateau measuring about
8 by 30 yards — has been up a steep slope; across the gully

---

[1] *Borlum* is old Gaelic for a ridge, and thus thoroughly descriptive of Dun Acha.

immediately to the north-west are some very large blocks of stone in regular line, evidently the remains of a defensive wall.

Dun Acha, to judge from the natural strength of its position, and the existence of numerous exterior buildings upon the lower ground, both to east and west, must have been an important fort. The occurrence of a slate whorl among the debris may also tend to show its comparatively late occupation. Pottery is plentiful (sometimes patterned [1]), and one small plain earthen cup, about 4 inches high and nearly complete, was in the possession of Mr. Darroch, the late factor; a small fragment was also found with a round hole pierced three-quarters of an inch below the rim, apparently for the purpose of the vessel's suspension. Broken pottery is common immediately under the turf, not more than 3 inches below the present surface. Many fragments of hammer-stones or 'pounders' were to be seen, and a very few complete specimens, including an implement (or weapon) bevelled off symmetrically for an inch or more at both the lower edges.[2] Colonel Stewart of Coll has a polishing stone which was found here, and flint-chips, although exceedingly scarce, also occur.

• 4   The next fort of this type is DUN COIRBIDH, about a mile to the south, upon Cnoc Coirbidh (locally pronounced 'Croc Horabi'),

---

[1] Patterned pottery was noticed in a number of the Duns, and probably could be found in almost all, if systematic digging were adopted. The types observed in Dun Acha are very generally characteristic, including a *raised* waved pattern close under the rim, and *incised* cross-lined and plain-lined, as also ruder markings evidently made by the nail of a finger or thumb.

[2] See annexed illustration, which is of the actual size.

DUN DUBH, FROM SOUTH-EAST.

DUN BEIC, FROM SOUTH-EAST.

a round knoll close to the shore at the east point of Frisland Bay. This knoll is very prominent, and upon its summit stands a single pillar stone—perhaps erected as a landmark for fishermen, although there are traces of a distinct ring of stones. To the south-east, near the base where the sandhill is broken, were found a few small pieces of pottery and a single flint. The surface of the Dun consists of smooth grass and does not therefore lend itself to further description, but the access was certainly from the west, where a walled winding path is clearly traceable up the steep side. In Frisland Bay is an ancient raised sea-beach, some 20 or 30 feet above the present high-water mark.

Frisland [1] farm-house is a quarter of a mile to the north-west, and in the tilled field, close to the front of the house, were noticed one or two flints with many fragments of old pottery. This latter was an unexpected find, and from a gravel-pit, about 200 yards north of the farm-house, another flint flake was obtained.

DUN GORTON,[2] nearly a mile to the west, is upon the eastern promontory of Loch Gorton, and near the farm-house of the same name. This fort occupies a very strong position upon overhanging rocks, immediately above the sea, but no more than its outlines are traceable, as it is completely overgrown by large and tenacious masses of sea-pink.

Passing, for the meantime, Carn a' Bhraighe (upon the peninsula of Fasachd), which is distinctly of another type, and the Marsh Dun near Breacacha, our next site is about two and a half miles

• 5

---

[1] *Frisland*, as a place-name, seems noteworthy.
[2] Locally pronounced 'Gorstian.' Gortan is Gaelic for a small field or garden.

• 6   north-west from Dun Gorton[1] upon the southern crest of BEN FOILL, where are the remains of a distinct Dun with walls at least a yard in width, both to the south-east and north-east. The turf is unbroken except at the northmost edge, where one small piece of pottery was found. Upon flattish ground, nearly half way down the declivity, are three cairns, one of them about 15 feet in diameter, but the other two only 3 feet across. In connection with these cairns it may be noted that the name of this head is Leac Chogaidh—'the (flat) stone of strife,' or perhaps 'the declivity of strife.'

    More than a mile north-east from the last mentioned, upon the crest of a large jutting cliff on the rocky coast west of
• 7   Totronald, is DUN BEIC.[2] Across its entrance — towards the east—stretches a massive natural rampart, which, however, has not improbably been artificially aided. The site is a very strong one, and upon the summit are scanty remains of several small separate buildings, in the centre of the westmost of which, by a little digging through the accumulated soil, were found numerous small round or oval stones averaging about an inch in length, such as occur plentifully upon many of the Duns in both Coll and Tiree. These water-worn pebbles are often flat-sided, while others resemble children's marbles; and it seems difficult to

---

[1] No Dun could be identified upon the south-west extremity of Coll—the peninsula of Caoles.

[2] Pronounced 'Veyik,' perhaps the Gaelic 'peak' or 'beak'; or possibly a proper name. Becc is mentioned as the head of a branch of Cinel Gabhran, who possessed the south half of Kintyre. He was killed A.D. 707, evidently in battle with his kinsmen of the Cinel Loarn (Skene's *Celtic Scotland*, second edition, vol. i. pp. 229, 273, 285).

explain their removal to a position so unnatural, unless they were carried thither for some special purpose.

Upon the south-west edge of the Dun, right upon the top of the cliff, were more of the same pebbles, together with many fragments of hammer-stones and pottery—some of the latter well patterned. The boundary walls are now practically non-existent, and this site yielded nothing further in the way of relics than two pieces of flint (rough and of poor quality), a material which is extremely scarce throughout the Duns of both islands.

A little to the east of TOTRONALD sandhills, about half a mile ●8 south from the summit of Ben Hogh, and a similar distance from the west shore, is an unnamed Dun. This was erected upon a small but precipitous rocky ridge, running north and south, and measuring about 78 by 55 feet over the enclosure. Two courses remain in part of the east wall, and the entrance, 4 feet wide, has been up the slope in this direction. The foundations are also to be traced upon the north end, although much grass-grown.

Next in order, nearly a mile to the north-west, and five hundred yards due west from BALLYHOGH farm-house, is another ●9 Dun, locally known as 'An Caisteal,' or *the castle*. This stood upon an elevated and much-denuded rock, near to (although not actually adjoining) the shore. Portions of its boundary-wall remain in three places on the south and south-west edges, as also to a less extent on the west and north. The rock is inaccessible except at this latter point. This site is within view of Dun Beic to the south, and Dun Foulag to the north. Only one or two doubtful hammer-stones were found here.

• 10   About half a mile east, upon the very summit of BEN HOGH, is another Dun, measuring about 18 by 21 feet, with its foundations still intact, but this was not visited by the writer.

Twelve hundred yards north-east from An Caisteal, upon an isolated rock of no great size and situated on the shore near the south point of Traigh Grianaig (marked 'Bagh Craimneach' on • 11   the Ordnance Map), is DUN FOULAG [1] (pronounced *Fulik*). Apart from its traditional name and the existence of slight walls to the south-east, where are also many fallen stones at the base, this Dun is not a well-marked site, although by no means of doubtful character. The rock is most abrupt, with a single access to the east, where the ascent is really a climb.

Upon a cliff very similar to that at Dun Beic, nearly half • 12   a mile north-east of Dun Foulag, stands the important DUN DUBH. It has been of considerable size and very strong, wholly inaccessible upon the west and south, which are sheer precipices. The rock runs east and west, almost opposite the skerry 'A' Mhuc,' and upon the east has been protected by an outer rampart, beyond which is to be seen part of a causeway of large stones by way of approach. Within the entrance are the foundations of two small contiguous buildings—probably guard-rooms— and still westward, traces of several others, although these are more indistinct. Many large stones have fallen, or have been thrown down, into the narrow gully to the south, as also at the steep north side, which latter, not being quite inaccessible, has had the additional protection of an outer wall half way down,

[1] *Faoileag* is Gaelic for 'a sea-gull.'

a portion of which still remains. The relics found were merely some poor hammer-stones and fragments of coarse pottery, together with small rounded pebbles, similar to those at Dun Beic. In a ravine, some thirty yards to the north, is a tiny rill, with, in its course, a heap of large stones, which have all the appearance of having formed a well in connection with the Dun.

The next site to be described is about two miles farther to the north-east. Here, upon RUDH' AN T-SEAN CHAISTEIL,[1] three-quarters of a mile west from Gallanach farm-house, has been a rock-fort, within sight of both Dun Dubh to the south-west and Dun Borbaidh to the north-east, about midway between the two, although nearer to Dun Dubh. The foundations of this 'old castle' can still be traced, but seem only to have been of about five yards internal diameter.

A mile to the east, in the second field beyond GALLANACH[2] farm-house, and half a mile from the nearest shore (Bagh na Trailleach), there has evidently been another Dun. This was

[1] 'The Point of the old Castle.'

[2] Gallanach may be *Gall-aonach*, 'the strangers' height.' Upon a neighbouring rocky hill, known as Cnoc Ghillibreidhe, are traces of ancient walls, and, as is elsewhere suggested, this name may possibly refer to the Earl Gilli who resided in Coll, *ca.* A.D. 980-1014, as scatt-collector for the then Earl of Orkney, or to one of his descendants. The name 'Gilli' would indicate that the Jarl was descended on the father's or more probably on the mother's side from that portion of the Gaelic tribes which had been subjected to the foreign rule. Some kind of stronghold may have existed upon the 'Cnoc.' According to local tradition 'a noble family' occupied this part in ancient times, their seat being known as 'Du-clach' (? Dun-clach). Two centuries after the time of Earl Gilli another Norse chief, Reginald (son of Godred, and king of the northern or Norwegian section of the Sudreys), had his chief residence in Coll, and was treacherously slain in 1229 (see Chapter XVI. on 'The Norwegian Occupation of the Hebrides').

not a rock-fort, but upon comparatively high arable ground. It now consists of two enclosures of large stones (that to the west measuring some 50 feet in diameter) containing the foundations of a number of small separate buildings, some circular but others apparently rectangular. Within the same field have recently been found two hammer-stones, one of them particularly well marked; but the site itself is a poor example, although of a distinct type.

Upon a rocky point on the north shore of Coll, two miles north-east from Gallanach, is DUN BORBAIDH. This spelling is taken from Eilean Borbaidh and Traigh Bhorbaidh, marked close to the Dun upon the Ordnance map; but the local pronunciation is *Borow* or *Borive*, differing materially from the map-name, which is probably incorrect. Indeed *Borive* bears a very close resemblance to the place-name *Borve*, which is not uncommon in the Outer Hebrides, appearing there to be merely a corruption of the Norse 'borg,' and to signify a fort, the word 'broch' being closely allied.

Although of but small extent, Dun Borbaidh[1] comes, together with Dun Acha, Dun Dubh, and Dun Anlaimh (in Loch nan Cinne-achan), among the four Coll forts of greatest present-day interest. From the south it has a long and straight cleared access (shown in the accompanying plate) upon the level between rocks, at first

[1] Dun Borbaidh shares the fate of many other Coll Duns, of most distinct character, in being quite unmarked upon the six-inch Ordnance Survey map. In fact it is simpler to put the matter conversely, and to state that only four (out of our twenty-nine) Forts and Carns in Coll are shown as ancient sites upon this large map. These exceptions are Dun Acha, Dun Beic, Carn a' Bhraighe, and the Marsh Dun at Poll nam Broig (Breacacha).

DUN BORBAIDH, FROM WEST. (SEE PP. 14-15.)

DUN BORBAIDH. FROM SOUTH.

very regular and about the width of a cart-road, but narrowing as the Dun is neared, with stepping-stones before it reaches the outer defences, composed of two low ramparts. From the existence of this evidently artificial approach and the character of much of the pottery (with many good patterns)[1] to be found upon the Dun itself, it would seem that this fort, although not large, has been of special importance. Small rounded pebbles are common, and hammer-stones also plentiful, many of them broken, and with evident marks of having been subjected to fire; in this respect notably resembling the condition of the foundations of Dun Acha. No flint seems to occur in Dun Borbaidh, but about a hundred yards south-east, upon a sandy break in the turf, was found a finely shaped flint scraper. Within the Dun near its entrance are some remains of a kitchen-midden.

Dun Borbaidh possesses no tradition, except in connection with a cave beneath it, entering from the rocky shore and reputed to extend far inland, which is said to have once been the scene of massacre of many natives.

At Bousd, a mile and a half east of Dun Borbaidh, upon a sandy knoll, immediately behind the mission-room, may be traced the foundations of a round, doubly-fenced erection. The interior circle is an enclosure of apparently 17 feet in diameter; the walls have evidently not been thick, and are about 40 inches apart. It is perhaps, however, incorrect to identify this site as

---

[1] The patterns on the pottery were much more varied than usual, including some which seem to be representations of fern-leaves, and another depicting a stag with only one antler shown.

that of a Dun, although the position is quite suitable—upon a triangular hillock, between two narrow streamlets which flow in very deeply worn gullies, uniting at the shore and there forming also the northern boundary.   Upon its surface is at least one kitchen-midden; flint-chips are common, together with a few scrapers, and there is abundance of rude unglazed pottery, a little of it patterned, generally of the simple sand-hill type.   Many small pieces of much corroded iron[1] are to be seen, including some rivets of the Viking type, such as were used for boats or chests.   Some years ago, after a severe storm, at least one bronze needle with a very large eye was found here, and it is believed that other objects of a similar period were also discovered.

Bousd will again be mentioned in connection with sandhill dwellings, which evidently have existed to the west, and also with a cemetery (apparently prehistoric), about 100 yards to the north.

Next follow four items more or less puzzling in character. Of these, the first seems to have been an ordinary Dun, although it is so thoroughly effaced as not to have been judged worthy of inclusion in a definite manner.   The most important evidence in its favour is the name of the hill upon which it stands— • 17   Cnoc na' Duin,[2] a slight elevation 300 yards north from Arinagour Inn, and about the same distance from the schoolhouse

---

[1] There was formerly a smithy where the mission-room now stands, which may account for much of the iron, although scarcely for the peculiar rivets, and *not at all* for the flint scrapers and patterned pottery.

[2] 'The hill of the Duns,' *plural*, thus denoting more than one fort.

on the west. Upon its summit is an unshapely mound with traces of a cairn in its centre, and a few loose stones in the surrounding turf. This is in a direct line between Carnan (No. 18) and the Island Dun in Loch Urbhaig (No. 25), both of them clearly within sight, together with an extensive general view. As above stated, the *name* of the hill forms the strongest evidence of its character, but it was the examination of the site itself that resulted in securing the name. Upon the summit of the hill—AN CARNAN [1]—a quarter of a mile south from Arinagour,   ● 18 are traces of an old structure upon an oval grassy mound, which measures about 21 by 13 feet, and contains some large stones upon its surface, the site being very noticeable amidst the surrounding heather. From this point are visible the island Duns in Loch an Duin to the north, and Loch Urbhaig to the east, as also the end of Loch Cliad (No. 27), and the fort upon the hill near Loch Boidheach (No. 2). Upon the slope to the east is a well, Tobar a' Charnain, but there is no suggestion of any connection between this and the structure upon the summit. Loch Airidh Meall Bhreide (now 'the Dairy Loch') is just below to the west; and upon the slope of the hill, between An Carnan and the loch, is pointed out the site of the ancient village of Arinagour, with many remains of walls and former cultivated enclosures. Towards the south end of Coll, upon the peninsula of Fasachd, between the sea-lochs Breacacha and Gorton (but much nearer the last named, and some 600 yards due west from Dun Gorton) is marked upon the Ordnance map CARN   ● 19

---

[1] 'The little cairn.'

A' BHRAIGHE.[1] This is a hollow stone building, the interior—
only about six feet in diameter—filled loosely with large stones,
and the whole most luxuriantly overgrown with nettles.   Carn
a' Bhraighe seems too small to have been a Dun (resembling
in this respect An Carnan), and may possibly prove to be a
chambered cairn.

• 20   There remain to be noticed two curious ridges of earth and
stones upon the island of GUNNA, off the south-west extremity
of Coll.   These are close to the mid-west shore of Gunna, at
Bagh Frachlan.   The smaller of the two crosses a gully (where
the stream now bisects it) at about ten yards from the beach,
and is some six feet in height, sloping towards the sea, but
abrupt on the inland side.   The second is upon level ground
a little to the north-east; about 3 yards in height, it extends
for nearly 100 yards north and south, the north end narrowed
and terminated by a large erect stone, but the south broken
away by a rude cart-track; the whole with the same characteristic
slopes as the smaller specimen.   About midway upon the landward edge of this ridge is a circular foundation, some 20 feet
in diameter over the walls.   A very little rude pottery was
found, but the site can hardly be described as a Dun—rather
as an earthwork with traces of a fort near its middle.

The island of Gunna is exactly a mile in length, rough and
hilly towards the west, level in part of the centre, and with
sandhills to the east; now tenanted only by Highland cattle
and a few goats.   At its west end is MacNeil's Bay, the

1 'The cairn of the brae.'

traditionary landing-place of the MacNeils of Barra, many of whom are said to have been there slain by the MacLeans of Coll. Near this bay is a large cairn, which may mark the grave of these MacNeils, but is more probably of prehistoric origin.

There was, perhaps, a Hill-Fort proper upon Gunna—on the high ground immediately to the north of the landing-place, Port na Cille.

As has been incidentally suggested, this list cannot be expected to be exhaustive. Almost without doubt other Hill-Forts existed (or yet exist) near the north-east shore, in the long stretch between Dulorichan and Loch Eatharna, and—to particularise—it seems highly probable that there were others immediately to the south of Cliad Bay, and to the north of Sorisdale, where indeed is the place-name Druim nan Carn. But, on account of the comparative absence of roads, Coll is a very awkward island to work, and it would require more than the four visits paid to it to examine all the localities which suggest themselves as likely sites. There may have been a Dun on the island of Ornsay, a mile south of Arina-gour, though a special visit did not reveal it.

The writer has recently noticed (upon a large map of Scotland, published by A. and C. Black) Dun Vinriff, marked upon the north coast of Coll, between Cornaig Beg and Cornaig Bay, near the Sloc na Luinge of the six-inch Ordnance Survey. This is about half a mile north-east from Dun Borbaidh and a very likely station for a Dun, but nothing can be added from personal observation, for which the hint came too late.

Class C

Loch or Marsh Duns—upon large mounds, and quite distinct from the Islet Duns of the next class.

This class is represented in Coll by only one specimen, while in Tiree four are to be found of manifestly the same type. Coll's single example is nearly a mile south of Breacacha, in the middle of a former loch (Poll nam Broig[1]) which was drained about the year 1875.[2] The mound is some 20 yards in diameter, with many stones, and also the appearance of natural rock on its surface. No relics were now to be seen, nor even the slightest trace of any built footway for access from the margin of the loch or marsh.

Duns upon Islets (usually artificial) in Fresh-Water Lochs.

These are somewhat numerous in Coll, but none are of any large area, and of none can the writer give a detailed account. All have evidently possessed 'clachans' or causeways[3] for approach, but of these very few are distinctly visible, except that to Dun Anlaimh in Loch nan Cinneachan, and the first section of another at the north end of Loch Cliad. Only two

---

[1] Evidently a modern name.

[2] During these draining operations was discovered the upper half of a bronze sword, pierced with four holes in the hilt. This sword is in Colonel Stewart's possession, and is mentioned in the *Proc. Soc. Antiq. Scot.*, vol. xii. p. 686.

[3] 'Causeways' may not be the best term for these clachans in connection with the Loch Duns. They are simply massive dry-stone dykes with flat tops a yard or more in width.

ISLAND DUN IN LOCH FADA, FROM WEST.

ISLAND DUN IN LOCH URBHAIG. FROM SOUTH.

of these islets are now accessible except by boat, and even if examination were thus made, they are so much overgrown by herbage or shrubs that an elaborate excavation would be necessary to give any results.

Commencing again at the north-east end of Coll, in the north of LOCH FADA (nearly a mile west from, and in view of, Dun Duloriohan), is a rather extensive Island Dun. It is some 20 yards from the shore, and appears to be at least 15 to 20 feet high, well covered by stunted saplings. The causeway was evidently from the north, where slight traces of it were identified at the water's edge. Within about a mile to the south of this, Loch Ronard (locally *Ronald*), Loch an t-Sagairt, and two others unnamed (three-quarters of a mile south of Loch an t-Sagairt), contain several islands, some of which may not improbably have been Duns, although the fact could not be definitely ascertained.

Near the south end of LOCH GHILLE-CALUIM,[1] about half a mile south of Loch Fada, is another Island Dun, to which in a dry summer access may be had by wading. This measures about 20 feet in diameter, with its wall still standing about 3 feet high towards the south.

Nearly half a mile north of Loch Ronard and close to the boundary fence between the 'Coll' and Cornaig estates, is a small reedy loch, only shown as a marsh upon the Ordnance

[1] Loch Ghille-Caluim is a fine sight at midsummer, the surface being then one large sheet of white water-lilies. The third chief of Clan MacLean was Malcolm,—Maol-Calum, or Gille-Calum,—who fought at Bannockburn, 1314 (MacLean's *History of the Clan MacLean*, p. 35).

• 24   Survey, though locally bearing the name of Loch Rathilt.[1] Near its north end is a long rocky island, upon which are the unmistakable remains of a Dun. This is 25 feet in diameter, the walls being 42 inches thick, with a causeway to the west and the actual entrance apparently to the east. Across a small point to the north on the opposite shore, facing the Dun, is a turf-covered wall about 3 feet thick and the same in present height, perpendicular towards the Dun, but sloping northwards —apparently an artificial screen, such as is afterwards noted at Loch Cliad.

• 25   In Loch Urbhaig, near Arivirig, only half a mile north from Arinagour across the long tidal inlet of Loch Eatharna (pronounced *Earna*) is an Island Fort, part of its walls distinctly traceable through the growth of bracken and royal-fern. There is said to be a causeway towards the north.

• 26   Near the north end of Loch an Duin (Loch of the Dun), about a mile north-west from Arinagour, is another definite site of similar character, which has been entirely surrounded by walls, those to the south and east being particularly distinct. This island contains natural rock, and is some 20 to 30 yards from the nearest shore. The causeway can be traced from the Dun to a separate low rock, and thence to a steep rocky point on the north-west shore of the loch, though it does not land there, but continues along the base of that rock to the level beach.

[1] Can this 'Rathilt' have any connection with the word 'Rath,' so common in Ireland as the native term for a Dun or Fort?

At both the north and south ends of LOCH CLIAD, half a mile farther north-west, are traces of buildings upon low, natural islands, in each case approached by a causeway. Loch Cliad is about half a mile long, but its level (and also consequently its area) has of late years been somewhat reduced by draining operations.

The site at the north end of the loch is much the better of the two. Here the island is approached by a curved causeway [1] some 3 yards wide at the shore end and 25 yards in length.

Eight or ten yards out the access is narrowed, and at this point a very large block of stone (8 ft. 6 in. by 2 ft. 9 in. by 2 ft.) lies across it—evidently placed there as a barrier. Upon the shore, whether to defend the causeway or with the object of screening both the flat island and the Islet Dun from the notice of enemies, are two separate earthworks, in line east and west, but with some interval between. [2] Of these the westmost is about 50 yards long and 9 feet high in the centre, abrupt to the south, but sloping to the north. The eastern mound

[1] This *curvature* of the causeways (which seems to be the usual, if not invariable, plan) may simply have been to give additional strength; but it suggests the idea that, when originally built, they did not quite reach the then surface of the water, with the result that while the rightful occupants of the Dun would make due allowance for the eccentricity, invaders or pursuers might be put to disadvantage. This theory seems quite compatible with the elevation of the causeways observed both in Coll and in North and South Uist. Add to this the statement made to the writer when in North Uist, that the practice was to place one or more large loosely-poised stones on the surface of the causeway, so as to give timely warning (through the clattering produced) in case of an attempted surprise by night.

[2] These screens would seem to indicate a native origin for the three distinct island sites in Loch Cliad.

is now considerably broken, and not nearly so distinct. The natural island itself is long and low, with the remains of a thick outer wall, and near its centre the foundations of several buildings—one of these apparently oval, and still showing two courses in parts. About 10 or 15 yards south-west is a much smaller islet of stones, to all appearance entirely artificial, and evidently once capped by a fort, the communication with which has been by way of the large flat island, where traces of a second causeway[1] are to be seen at the nearest point to the Dun. It is this smaller island for which the west mound no doubt mainly acted as a mask.

Coming to the south end of Loch Cliad, there is a much poorer repetition of causeway and natural island, together with a single earthwork on the opposite shore, only in this case the mound or screen is in more perfect condition than either of those at the north end. It is (as may be expected) abrupt to north and sloping to south, thus reversing the arrangement which holds near the better causeway, on account of the altered relative positions of island and mound. Its measurements are some 60 yards in length by 11 in width at the centre (including the whole of the outer slope), but narrowing towards both ends, the greatest height being only about 6 feet. There are but scanty traces of a causeway to the flat island, which is somewhat similar to the intermediate one, already described, at the north end of

[1] The protective arrangements are specially elaborate in this case. In the first place two ramparts on the shore; then a curved causeway (with a huge stone obstructing it) to the intermediate island; and finally a second causeway from the larger to the smaller island.

ISLAND DUN IN LOCH AN DUIN, FROM EAST. (SEE P. 22.)

the loch. Here are the foundations of a circular building of about 3 yards interior diameter, with inner and outer walls 2 feet apart, and again at an interval of some yards, another and wider concentric wall. A little to the north are further traces of several buildings, with some large stones. An interesting feature is the occurrence, in the water off the north extremity of this island, of two large rings of stones, one of them nearly adjoining the north point (in the then low level of the loch), and the second about 20 yards further out, giving the appearance as if of a series of forts in the middle of the loch, in a line north and south.

Each of the Upper and Lower Mill Lochs—marked upon the Ordnance map Loch nan Cinneachan and Loch Anlaimh—contains an Island Dun. The Gaelic names of these lochs, as of the islets (Eilean nan Cinneachan and Eilean Anlaimh), are most suggestive, meaning the loch and island 'of the heathen (or Gentiles)'[1] and 'of Olaf' respectively. Locally, the island-fort in Loch nan Cinneachan (the Upper Mill Loch) is known as DUN ANLAIMH, which may seem contradictory, although as ● 28 a matter of fact the two lochs have probably once formed one only, and indeed even now are scarcely separated, except for a highly raised roadway which crosses between them. The head of Loch nan Cinneachan is fully two miles west from Arina-gour, and both of the narrow lochs taken together are about a mile in length, lying north and south. Dun Anlaimh is near the north end of the upper loch, and perhaps 20 to 30 yards

---

[1] In the Irish Annals the Norsemen are styled 'Gentiles.'

from the east shore, whence it is approached by a well-preserved causeway through rather deep water. A grassy mound crowns the loose stones which form the apparently artificial islet, and the foundations of buildings are clearly traceable. Upon the brow of a hill which is close to the west of the loch—Cnoc nan Tota, 'the hill of the dwellings'—and overlooking the Dun, are the remains of two pairs of circular erections ; and again, on the east side, and farther south—just opposite the elevated roadway which now divides the upper and lower lochs—is the site of another and larger round building.

● 29   In the LOWER MILL LOCH, about half way down its east side, and not in shallow water, is another evidently artificial island with signs of a former Dun. This island is about twice as far from the shore as that in the upper loch, and no causeway is visible, though one is said to exist.

Concerning the first of these two island-forts,—Dun Anlaimh, in the Upper Mill Loch,—there runs a somewhat detailed tradition to the effect that in it lived the Norse chief who held Coll long after the neighbouring islands had been abandoned by his comrades. It is said that MacLean of Duart already possessed Tiree, and that one of his sons determined to attack the Norseman (presumably an *Olaf*) in this islet stronghold. The Norwegians, finding themselves overcome, threw their weapons into the loch, to put these beyond the reach of their victors. A precise date, the year 1384, is even attached to the story, although it is well to confess that this chronology is reached from the fact that the MacLeans of Coll sold their possessions in that island in 1856, and, according to their family records, had then held them for 472 years.[1]   Hence the only too simple retrospective calculation !

Another version of evidently the same incident (not seen until after the above had been received *viva voce*) is contained in the Rev. J. G. Campbell's[2] *Clan Traditions and Popular Tales* (p. 7) : 'The Laird of Dowart was on his way to gather rent in Tiree and sent ashore to Kelis, Coll, for meat. The woman of the house told MacLean was not worth sending meat to, and Dowart kindly came ashore to see why she said so. She said it because he was not taking Coll for himself. Three brothers from Lochlin[3] had Coll at the time, Annla Mor in Loch Annla, another in Dun Bithig in Totronald, and the third

---

[1] The traditional date above quoted may be sufficiently well founded, so far as concerns the earliest historical record of a MacLean (Lachlan Makgilleone) holding possession of *Tiree* and the Treshnish Isles (*constabulariam et custodiam castrorum de Kernaborg . . . officium ballivatus totarum terrarum de Tyriage cum terris infrascriptis, viz., unciata terre de Mannawallis, et dimedia unciata terre de Hindebollis*) by charters from his brother-in-law, Donald, second Lord of the Isles, of date 12th July 1390, which were confirmed by James I., and again in July 1495 by James IV. (*Reg. Mag. Sig.*)   But as regards the island of *Coll*, the first authentic notice (*anno* 1409) of a MacLean connection that we have been able to discover is included in the same confirmation of 1495, and merely refers to '*terras 6 marcarum de Tyrvnghafeal in insula Cola, loco victualium farrine et casei ab incolis de Tyriage . . . prius annuatim dari consueti,*' and this in connection with the constabulary of Cairnburg.   John MacLean (surnamed 'Garbh') is said to have been the first of Coll, and his date would seem to be from somewhere about 1450 (MacLean's *History of the Clan MacLean*, pp. 45-47, and Gregory's *History*, p. 71).   These matters are however discussed in some detail in Chapter VII., 'Coll—Its Clan History,' and Chapter VIII., 'The Treshnish Isles.'   The MacLeans did not hold Tiree for quite three centuries, that island passing in 1674 to the Argyll family, with whom it still remains.

[2] A former parish minister of Tiree, who died in 1891.

[3] Norway.

in Grishipol hill. She had thirty men herself fit to bear arms. Dowart went to Loch Annla fort late in the evening alone and was hospitably received. Annla's arrows were near the fire, and Dowart gradually edged near them till he managed to make off with them. This led to a fight at Grimsari, and is perhaps the reason why Dowart encouraged Iain Garbh to make himself master of Coll.'

The forts here mentioned are Dun Anlaimh (in the Upper Mill Loch), Dun Beic at Totronald, and Dun Dubh in Grishipol. There probably was a battle fought near Totronald, and within a mile of Grimisary, the place being still known as Sruthan nan Ceann, or 'The Burn of the Heads.'[1] Whether or not there may be, in these stories about Dun Anlaimh, some confusion between the Norsemen and the MacNeils of Barra, as the enemies whom young MacLean of Duart defeated, the clearly defined and well preserved causeway (in deep water) to this Dun in the Upper Mill Loch, would lead to the conclusion that it was one of the island forts last to be abandoned.

Although King Magnus IV. of Norway surrendered the Hebrides to Scotland in 1266 (after the battle of Largs), it seems certain that many of his vassals and their descendants would continue to occupy their property (and also their strongholds) in these islands far at least into the next century, even if it is to be supposed that the Scottish Kings received any real submission from the aliens in remote and (to this day) unfre-

---

[1] This battle, however, seems not to have been fought until 1596, two hundred years later. See *postea*.

quented parts like Coll, without a delay of very many years. One of the articles of the treaty of 1266 provided that the then resident Norsemen should be at liberty either to go or remain, those who made the latter choice becoming Scottish subjects.

CHAPTER III

COLL—HUT CIRCLES (INLAND)

THIS is a type represented by perhaps four large specimens in Coll, all situated somewhat inland and three of them at a considerable distance from any well-defined fort, while the absence of outer defences makes them appear to bear the character of native[1] dwellings. They do not exceed about 6 yards' interior diameter, with turf (or mixed stone and turf) walls now not over 3 or 4 feet in height.

By far the best example stands on a hill-slope three-quarters of a mile north of Arinagour, on the further side of the stream which enters Loch Eatharna, and about 300 yards east from the mission-house. Here is one large round and very green knoll with two smaller mounds close to it on the west. The larger knoll is 10 or 12 feet high with the remains in its centre of an erection 6 yards in diameter, surrounded by an outer wall (of which only the foundations show) enclosing a total area of some 18 yards across. The smaller knolls are respectively about 6 and 4 yards in diameter, and from 3 or 4 feet to half of that in height. This group is the only one which it was attempted

---

[1] According to the local tradition, the natives were driven *inland* by the Norsemen. Indeed it is more than probable that—by whomsoever erected—the Hill-Forts, if not also the Islet Duns, would in most cases be occupied or appropriated by the invaders during the Viking supremacy.

to test by means of a little digging, fortunately with some definite (if slender) results. In the side of the largest mound were disclosed fragments of rude, unglazed pottery (one piece with a simple pattern) and in the smaller ones, kitchen-midden refuse, shells, fish-bones, and clayey ashes, with a very few fragments of flint—all about a foot below the present surface. Indeed it was much like probing an inferior specimen of the Hill-Forts, the chief distinctions being the total absence of hammer-stones, and—an important point—the slender nature of the outer barrier which encircles the larger knoll. Judging by the nature of the pottery, etc., found in it, this ruin would appear to date from about the same period as that of the later occupation of the forts proper.

Upon the point between Port na Luinge and Crossapol Bay (some 200 yards south of the MacLean Mausoleum) are two considerable mounds to which no local name is attached. Flint chips and a few fragments of pottery were also found here, but the remains are too scanty to afford any satisfactory classification.

About 400 yards south-east of Kilbride farmhouse are the ruins of one large and three smaller round erections. These however do not possess the same knoll-like character, but have stone walls and stand upon an elevated plateau.

Again, upon the east side of Loch nan Cinneachan, opposite the raised roadway which now divides the Upper and Lower 'Mill' Lochs, are the foundations of a large circular building.

Upon the steep hill-side, 200 yards south of Loch a Mhill

Aird Beg, is a group of four round or oval erections, one of them considerably larger than the others.

But indeed, with the exception of the first mentioned (near Loch Eatharna) and next in degree, that near Loch nan Cinneachan, it may be safer to assume that most of these circular remains are merely ruins of an old type of croft. Several smaller round erections were noticed, especially towards the east end of Coll, in very remote parts near Loch Ghille-Caluim and Loch an t-Sagairt, occurring as distinct knolls and in pairs, or in groups of three or four. Similarly four others of a like shape, although not of the knoll character, are to be found on the north slope of Carnan Dubha, just above Loch an Duin; and at Cnoc nan Tota ('the hillock of the dwellings'), immediately to the west of Loch nan Cinneachan and looking down upon its island fort (Dun Anlaimh), is another row of four, in pairs. All these were probably an early type of shieling, the Gaelic word for this—Airidh—entering very largely into the place-names in the northern half of the island. The various Airidhs marked upon the Ordnance map in Coll are literally too many to enumerate, although it would seem that it is many years since any were in actual occupation. Shielings are still in use in Lewis, and the writer counted in 1901 over a dozen (of oblong shape and turf-roofed) in view together at one point within twelve miles from Stornoway. South of Loch Roag, upon the last-named island, groups of ruined shielings, of circular form, are not rare, but the dimensions of those examined ran to only 8 or 9 feet of internal diameter.

COTTAGE AT GRISHIPOL.

As has already been stated, the population of Coll is now only one-third of what it was in the middle of the eighteenth century. Throughout the island are to be found the ruins of numerous (more or less rectangular) deserted cottages or crofts. Of these little special notice has been taken, although sometimes a curious and distinctive type was observed; for instance one with a massive curved stone porch, and another with double south walls (4 feet apart) on Carnan Dubha, south of Loch an Duin.

A little north of Loch Eatharna a substantial ruin was noted, containing a central paved hearth about 2 feet in diameter, flanked midway towards each gable by a short and low symmetrical stone wall—these dwarf walls seeming to have served as two fixed benches or settles facing the fireplace.

CHAPTER IV

COLL—SANDHILL DWELLINGS

In Coll, as in Tiree, ancient hearths and kitchen-middens occur in many large groups, and are almost invariably to be traced in any spot where the sandhills are much blown, that is to say, as a general rule, near the northern and western shores of both islands.

Hammer-stones are almost as plentiful in connection with this class as in the ancient Forts, and the same may be said with regard to the abundance of fragments of pottery. The character, however, of the pottery found upon the sandhills usually differs materially from that yielded by the Duns, being almost invariably of a ruder or more gravelly nature, while the few patterns to be observed upon it are small and simple in the extreme, being in this way so distinctive as to make it seem easy to decide at sight whether a piece of patterned pottery comes from a Dun or a sandhill. An even more noteworthy contrast exists in the large quantities of flint-chips which are to be found in connection with the present class, especially as flint is exceedingly rare in all the Duns that were examined.

These facts would make it appear that the sandhills were occupied either at a different epoch or by another people from

FLINT SCRAPERS FROM COLL SANDHILLS, ACTUAL SIZE.

FLINT ARROW-HEADS AND IMPLEMENTS FROM COLL SANDHILLS,

(ONE FROM TIREE), ALL ACTUAL SIZE.

those to be associated with the Duns—in all probability at an *earlier* period, and evidently by a *native* race.

Indeed, to hazard a theory which would have some (although admittedly inconclusive) support, it might be suggested that the sandhill dwellings—all of them without any evidence of real defences—were inhabited by the lower order of natives before the Vikings made the Hebrides their annual hunting-ground.[1]

Plentiful as these sites of dwellings are, many more must be hidden under the high, bent-covered mounds of drifted sand, and it may be that only a small proportion are now to be traced, their exposure varying from year to year according to the wind which most prevails.[2]

As regards the structures themselves, not more than the merest outlines of any remain, but they were certainly circular, with an average diameter of perhaps 8 to 12 yards, a measurement which has usually to be *estimated* on account of the great obliteration.

It has already been mentioned that the sandhill dwellings occur in groups, often very extensive. The first site to be noticed is at BOUSD, at the north-east of Coll; to the west

---

[1] Although the first historic notice of the Vikings in the Hebrides dates back only to the eighth or ninth century, it seems probable that this would by no means be their first appearance upon our shores. When (and if) the twenty-nine Duns (of various types) which we enumerate for Coll were occupied at one and the same time, it would not seem too much to say that these alone would be capable of housing a population of at least 500 individuals at the lowest computation.

[2] As in Tiree, pottery (often with fragments of much corroded iron) is to be found in almost every part of Coll where the turf above the sand is broken, and this in spots far distant from any present or other traceable cottage.

of the Dun (No. 16)—already described as situated upon a triangular hillock, between two deeply-worn gullies—is strewn a quantity of pottery (a little of it patterned), with flints, including some scrapers.[1] There are, however, no well-defined sites, except several kitchen-middens with ashes, shells, and bones; a few horses' teeth and scraps of iron are also met with.

About 100 yards to the east, upon lower ground just above the beach, is a spot almost covered with large stones. Here was noticed one good hammer-stone, but very little pottery, and no flint. Possibly this has been an ancient cemetery. Still farther to the north-east, always near the shore, a little pottery was found at intervals as far as the point Rudh' an t' Ard Eiridh. At TOROSTAN, about two miles south-west of Bousd (passing on the way a little pottery in broken sandhills by the side of the very rough road or track), is a much more extensive series of sites scattered over a large flat area dotted with small mounds. This is a little south of Dun Borbaidh, and immediately east of the burn which flows out of Loch a' Mhill Aird and forms a boundary between the Coll and Cornaig estates.[2] The local name is 'Uchd na Carn,' meaning 'the breast of the Cairns,' and the remains are of a mixed character (perhaps both dwellings and burials), as indeed is the case with many

---

[1] Half of a well-shaped stone axe—a long oval—was found here. The flints are of good quality, and do not appear to occur naturally in Coll, nor indeed in any district near.

[2] The central portion, by far the largest division of Coll (the former possession of the MacLeans) is owned by Colonel Stewart. The two ends of the island, Caoles to the south-west and Cornaig to the north-east, now belong to the Buchanan family, although these intermediately formed part of the large domains of the Dukes of Argyll.

of the sandhill sites, both in Coll and Tiree. This is especially marked at Bousd and Torostan, in the northern part of Coll, as also at Cliad and Totronald, where burials and dwelling-sites occur very near each other, although presumably of quite different epochs, separated in this respect, it may be, by many centuries. At Torostan, for example, is one large heap about 6 yards in diameter at the top, and some 15 feet high, with the appearance of a circularly built chamber in its centre, the top of which, indeed, was partly open in the summer of 1896, although by next year it had been closed. This site is evidently that of a very old burial—a chambered-cairn [1]—but only 40 yards to the north stands a relic of very different nature, an exceedingly large kitchen-midden, which is simply a mass of limpet-shells, interspersed by a few coarse periwinkles, bones, and broken stones, without a fragment of pottery to be seen. Close to the chambered-cairn rude pottery was plentiful (some of it in large pieces, but very little patterned) together with several hammer-stones. Flint is very scarce, but to the east a few good scrapers were found, also a leaf-shaped arrow-head and an imperfect barbed one—very rare items. Indistinct sites of buildings are common towards the south and east, and there seem also to have been some cists. A disc of stone, the size of one's palm, quite flat upon one side, was picked up, the centre of the flat side indented as if by use.

A mile south-west of Torostan, upon the GALLANACH sand-hills beyond Killunaig churchyard, a little pottery was seen,

---

[1] The chambered-cairn is a most ancient burial type, dating back to the remote stone age.

especially among the lofty sand-slopes just to the west of the chapel. There are distinct ashes in one place (although the site is not otherwise to be identified as a dwelling) with pottery (some simply patterned), but hammer-stones and flints are hardly to be found. Southwards, towards Gallanach, is a single opened cist, containing human bones, and near it further remains of what have probably also been cists; others have certainly been found. Farther on are several heaps of stones, with pottery sometimes near them; but without doubt most of the ancient sites here are covered by the high sandhills, or hidden by the strongly growing bents on lower ground. Near this place have recently been found a short bone pin with a large round head, a pen-annular bronze ring, and a brass pin of old (though probably not ancient) make; also a pin formed of bronze wire with twin loops at its head. Close to the east of the path —for it is hardly a road—between Bousd and Gallanach, more pottery is to be seen, together with corroded iron, nails, and rivets, but much cannot be made of this iron, lying as it does so near the regular track to the east end of the island.

South of Gallanach and Arinabost, among the CLIAD sand-hills, between the road and the sea, is an extensive tract of broken sand, containing many comparatively level spaces. Here,[1]

[1] About the year 1880 a fine pen-annular bronze brooch was found at Cliad, although it is erroneously described by Mr. Donald Ross (*Proc. Soc. Antiq. Scot.*, vol. xv. p. 153) as from Traigh Foill. This brooch is in the possession of Colonel Stewart of Coll, and was exhibited by him to the Society, in whose *Proceedings* it is figured (vol. xv. p. 80). In diameter it measures about 1½ inches, with a loose pin nearly 3 inches long. 'The brooch, which is covered with a fine green patina, is of the usual form of a Celtic brooch of the late Christian period (ninth to twelfth century), viz., a flattened band of equal width, expanding at the ends,

hammer-stones were specially common, and occasionally very large ; a bone borer, thick at one end and well pointed at the other, a little pottery (including simple patterns chiefly of plain or dotted lines), and a few flints, including scrapers, were also found. Only in one spot, close to a small kitchen-midden, was flint at all plentiful, a chief feature of the Cliad sandhills being the abundance of well-marked hammer-stones.

Near the northern limit is a building within a mound, probably a chambered-cairn similar to that at Torostan, but nothing special could be noted except that it appears to have contained two closely adjacent cells (which seem to have been opened in recent years), and two or three pieces of flint were found near.

A little south of Cliad Burn, and upon higher ground, are several groups of large stones, apparently the remains of dwellings (or less probably of burials), but almost nothing was to be discovered south of this burn, as the hillocks there change their character, and are more rounded (perhaps even rocky), besides being mostly covered with bents or turf.

Still farther south, upon the slopes above GRISHIPOL Bay, are other interesting sites with a number of good hammer-stones, but comparatively little pottery or flint. The best of these is that situated farthest from the shore, with a distinct kitchen-

on which a long pin moves loosely by a loop. There is a square socket for a setting (now gone) in the centre of the ring of the brooch, and two circular settings of green glass (one of which is gone) are at the junctions of the ring with the expanded part of the brooch. On each of the flattened expansions there are five circular settings of green glass of smaller size. The whole surface of the expanded part is covered with a peculiar ornament, produced by cross-hatching the surface deeply with a graver, and then gilding it ' (*Ibid.*).

midden of much-decayed periwinkle and limpet shells, a little pottery, and an occasional hammer-stone.

Two miles south-west of Grishipol are the extensive sand-flats, lying between the farmhouses of Ballyhogh and TOTRONALD. East of the track (road there is none, for more than a mile across these loose sands) are several sites marked by groups of stones. The largest of all is nearest to the road, and consists of a distinct mound, measuring some 12 by 13 yards, with two large stones upon its summit and many strewn upon its surface, while horse-bones occurred in some quantity. Similar sites extend eastward into hidden hollows among the sandhills, and of these two were found to be respectively a circle of 25 feet diameter, and an oval of 25 by 35 feet. All of these were disappointing in the way of relics, but fragments of pottery and broken flints (hammer-stones being almost absent) at least attest some ancient characteristics — probably as cemeteries, especially since the sites are quite separate, not continuous like the sandhill dwellings.

Westward from the track, the sands present a most curious appearance, the surface of the small heaps having formed itself into many isolated table-tops of firm consistency, almost as if petrified. These are called the 'frozen' sands, and evidently contain a large proportion of lime, doubtless from powdered or decayed shells.

At the extreme south (or Totronald) end is at least one large kitchen-midden of shells, bones, and pottery, with a number of horses' teeth lying about. Flint is here abundant,

SANDHILL-SITE NEAR TRAIGH FOILL.

SANDHILL-SITE (CAUSEWAYS) NEAR TRAIGH FOILL.

including a few scrapers, and pottery is also common, although both these classes become much scarcer towards the north. Distinct hammer-stones occur, and several good pins have been found, including a fine one of bronze, short and rather blunt, engraved across its centre and head, and with a small round flat recess on the very top, which has evidently held a piece of either glass or enamel. Another pin was of bone, and a third of brass, precisely similar to that which has been described as from Gallanach.

About a mile and a half south-west from Totronald, occupying the isthmus (fully half a mile wide) between TRAIGH FOILL and Crossapol Bay, are numerous and most interesting sites. Those best marked are towards the south, comprising especially one large circle of about 12 yards diameter upon a slight mound of sand, covered with loose stones, some of which are of considerable size, and having upon its surface many flints (some of them scrapers) and fragments of coarse pottery (seldom patterned[1]), with a few bones bearing the appearance of having been in use as domestic implements. There occur also some hammer-stones, both complete and broken, and a few polishing-stones, although these latter are rather undefined as to purpose. The same site includes a kitchen-midden of bones and shells, out of which was dug a long and well-shaped bone bodkin.

A little to the north-east were more flints, pottery, and a few pieces of iron, near another kitchen-midden heap, with bones

[1] Two fragments with thick rims are probably of funeral urns. One is distinctly marked with small circles, as if by the end of a rush, *inside*; the other has small round indentations and short lines outside, with transverse lines also upon its inner bevelled edge.

and the distinct marks of fire. Near this spot was found a large bone needle, the size of its head showing the necessity for the use, along with it, of a borer or bodkin such as has just been described as found some 200 yards to the south-west. Not far from this needle were two stone sinkers and what seemed to be a stone axe of greenish material, well shaped but much weather-worn.

Northwards from this site are the remains—very clearly defined—of a long, rectangular stone wall, or more probably causeway. Indeed it seems as if there had existed here an extensive lake-village (although not of the Crannog type), the dwellings apparently connected by causeways, and the whole covering a great portion of the southern half of the isthmus. The causeway in question runs north from the middle of one heap of stones to another, then north again, afterwards turning west at right angles.

In the northern half of this low-lying flat are a few specimens of the fantastic table-topped sandhills, such as have been described between Ballyhogh and Totronald, but towards this part both pottery and flints practically cease to occur.

In *Blackwood's Magazine* of August 1882 is an article [1] entitled 'Some Glimpses of the Prehistoric Hebrideans,' which describes this lake-village near Crossapol Bay, and mentions two bronze ornaments as there found—a brooch and a pin [2]— the former and the finer of the two being in reality from Cliad, as already noted.

[1] By Mr. Donald Ross, Inspector of Schools.
[2] The pin is figured in *Proc. Soc. Antiq. Scot.*, vol. xv. p. 81.

Near the south-west extremity of Coll, at CAOLES, about 100 yards from the shore and just to the west of the telegraph wire which there passes from Coll to Tiree, is another (apparently single) site in a sandhill among the bents. Here were fully 10 yards of a semicircular wall traceable as the east side of a building, with ashes, hammer-stones,[1] flints (including four scrapers), some pottery (none patterned), a piece of iron slag, and a horse's bone and tooth. A quarter of a mile to the east, upon the other side of the telegraph-line and about equi-distant with the last from the shore, is another much larger break in the turf above massive, out-cropping rock. Close above the rock in many places was a soft earthy iron slag, some of it in a tubular form amongst ashes, but all of it evidently waste. One flint was found here, also two hammer-stones and a little pottery.[2]

Half a mile north-west from the signal-post of the telegraph cable, at the north end of TRAIGH NA SIOLAG, in a sandy recess above the beach, is part of a strongly-built semicircular wall, some 3 feet high, with a slight batter, and 5 yards in con-tinuous length, more of it being just traceable. This is evidently a raised sandhill dwelling, especially as in its centre, at a little higher level, a kitchen-midden is disclosed. Among the refuse was found a bone with a symmetrical hole bored through its thicker end, and also some pottery, including a single fragment

[1] One small hard hammer-stone was very peculiar, with many deep scratches upon its sides.

[2] This spot is marked on the Ordnance map as *Bàcan Seileach*, which seems to mean the hollows or sand-dunes of the willows.

patterned with the simple type of the sandhills. In addition
to these were observed a few fragments of flint and iron slag,
and a horse's tooth, together with one or two poor hammer-
stones.

A quarter of a mile still farther west (also just above the
shore) are several stone heaps upon a sandy slope—otherwise
a most unsatisfactory site, although a single bit of pottery was
found there.

Immediately to the east of Ben Foill, above Port an t-Soair,
is a small sand-break with a kitchen-midden and some pottery.
Although a genuine ancient site, modern pottery is here inter-
mingled, evidently from two ruined cottages not far off.

Another site of somewhat different type may also be noticed.
This is a mile from the nearest shore and about half way between
Arileod and Totronald, literally upon the side of the road, which
cuts through it. Here has been a large kitchen-midden of
limpets and periwinkles, with a few bones. The neighbouring
soil is not at all sandy, and about 150 yards to the north (close
to the west of the road) is a gravel-pit containing numerous
flaked flints, one of which proved to be a fashioned scraper.

CHAPTER V

COLL—PREHISTORIC BURIAL-SITES

IN the preceding chapter incidental notice has been taken of several burials, presumably pagan, both separately and in groups, upon the sandhills of BOUSD, TOROSTAN, GALLANACH, CLIAD, and TOTRONALD, as nearly associated with ancient dwellings, and these are therefore not again here detailed. But the most remarkable site, and that an evidently pre-Christian enclosed cemetery, is upon a hillock called CNOC A' BHADAIN[1] (not marked on the Survey map) a hundred yards south of the mission-house at Braloch, and nearly a mile north of Arinagour. Here is a large and comparatively level walled area, 15 yards in diameter, still containing two broken cists (both lying approximately north and south) together with the apparent remains of a number of others. Stones are strewn over the enclosure, but the largest have evidently been removed for building purposes, whether to a now ruined cottage close to the north, or for the mission-house itself.

[1] We can offer no explanation of this name, except that (Skene's *Celtic Scotland*, second edition, vol. i. pp. 145, 228, 264) 'the most northerly part of Dalriada was the small state called Cinel Baedan, or Kinel-vadon, which was a part of the larger tribe of the Cinel Eochagh, one of the three subdivisions of the Cinel Loarn, but separated from the rest by . . . Linnhe Loch' (the south part of Morvern being given as its exact position), Baedan having been son of Eochaidh, the grandson of Loarn Mor; and further that a *Mons Badonicus* was besieged in A.D. 516.

A quarter of a mile north-west of ARINABOST are portions of an irregularly shaped mound standing north and south, in which were found, it is stated, a bronze weapon and what was called a helmet, together with small square scales supposed to be of armour.

Fifty yards north of Grishipol farmhouse, adjoining the west side of the road, is a small mound, with an outside diameter of 15 feet, inside 7½ feet. This burial cairn, according to local tradition, was opened about the year 1765 [1] by three Norwegians (or strictly, 'by three men from Lochlinn,' which may mean either Denmark or Norway) in the presence of Mr. Hugh MacLean, then laird of Coll. It is added that the strangers took home with them the relics disclosed, claiming these to pertain to a fellow-countryman, if not even an ancestor. It is a curious story, and one wonders how the Norwegians could feel so sure of the identity of their kinsman. This is the 'CARNAN MHIC AN RIGH' incidentally mentioned by the Rev. J. G. Campbell. [2]

A little to the south of TOTRONALD farmhouse, and close to the east of the road, in a level space upon an eminence, are two large upright stones, marked upon the Ordnance map as ' Remains of Stone Circle.' From their relative positions it seems evident that these stones never formed part of any circle, and a more probable explanation (agreeing also with local tradition) is that they are ancient burial-marks. The two stones stand north and south, 46 feet apart. That to the north is gable-shaped,

[1] The excavation is stated to have taken place before Dr. Johnson's visit to Coll in 1773.

[2] *Clan Traditions and Popular Tales*, p. 9.

STANDING STONES AT TOTRONALD.

showing about 5 feet above ground, with a very slight mound to its south.   The other is of more irregular form, and 6 feet in height.

Upon the very summit of Ben Foill are the remains of a Cist, one end and side being in position, together with other fallen stones.

There is said to be another Cist upon Beinn Tuiridh (the hill of mourning), north of Loch Ballyhogh, but this site was not verified.

In the island of Ornsay, upon the centre of a ridge which seems to be an ancient raised sea-beach formed by the action of the waves, is a very large cairn which probably covers a pre-historic burial.

At the north-east corner of Loch Ghille-Caluim, just above the water's edge, is another large cairn, consisting of loose stones greatly overgrown by heather, covering an extent of at least 4 by 3 yards.

CHAPTER VI

COLL—PRE-REFORMATION CHAPELS AND BURIAL-GROUNDS

DR. REEVES, in his excellent monograph upon the ancient ecclesiastical remains of Tiree,[1] briefly enumerates eleven Chapels as having formerly existed in Coll and Gunna. This list the present writer has attempted to verify, succeeding, thanks to much local aid, except in two instances, those of Caoles (No. II.) and Arintluich (No. IX.), of the first of which it is significant to note that Dr. Reeves wrote in 1854,—'the foundations of a chapel and the traces of a cemetery are still visible.' Thus easily do ancient sites disappear, since neither by tradition nor observation could any definite trace be found at Caoles.

For convenience of reference, Dr. Reeves' numeration is here followed :—

+I   First mentioned is the island of GUNNA, with 'the remains of a chapel and cemetery. It was exclusively the burial-place of the MacNeills[2] of Coll.'

The church is still distinctly traceable above Port na Cille, near the south-east corner of Gunna, and the best landing-place

[1] *Ulster Journal of Archæology*, October 1854, pp. 243 and 244. The Coll stations are not described from the personal observation of Dr. Reeves (as was the case in Tiree), the list being given him by 'Mr. Lachlann MacQuarrie, the Duke of Argyll's ground-officer in Tiree.'

[2] *MacNeill* appears to be an error for *MacLean*, no doubt caused by some confusion with MacNeil's Bay, already mentioned as at the west end of Gunna.

in that island.   Upon the grassy slope, half way up from the
harbour, is a good spring, evidently the chapel-well.

'At CAOLES, opposite to Gunna, the foundation of a chapel   +II
and the traces of a cemetery are still visible.'

This site, as already stated, could not now be determined, unless
it was immediately to the north of Port an Duine, where are
the remains of some characterless east and west building.

At CROSSAPOL, close to the farmhouse and between it and   +III
the shore, is a churchyard, one of the two still used for burials in
Coll, the second being at Killunaig.   This is close to the sea, and
indeed at its south side the graveyard is gradually diminishing,
as the rocks below give way.   According to Dr. Reeves' account,
the foundations of the chapel were to be seen sixty years ago,
but now no trace can be observed, probably on account of the
very uneven surface of the burying-ground and the strong growth
of herbage.   Another writer[1] in 1861 agrees that no traces of the
chapel then remained, but speaks of 'the shaft of a sculptured
cross of great beauty,' which, however, was not to be found in
1896-99.   Of mediæval slab-stones of the Iona type, only two were
observed, one of them much defaced, and the other sculptured with
a two-handed sword, floriated ornament, and figures of animals.

At Breacacha 'was a chapel, with its cemetery, called   +IV
ARDNEISH ; but about eight years ago[2] the tenant removed the
ruins for building purposes, and put the disused cemetery under
tillage.'   This statement seems entirely correct, the chapel

---

[1] Muir, in his *Characteristics of Old Church Architecture, etc.*, p. 151.

[2] That is, *ca.* 1846.

probably having stood about a mile south-west from the old Castle of Breacacha, immediately to the south of the modern square erection known as 'MacLean's Mausoleum.' This is within half a mile of a small bay named Port Aoir Ard-innis, without doubt identical with 'Ardneish.'

+V

'At Breachachadh also, on the east side of the farm called FASACH, is the ruin of a chapel with a burial-ground, which was used within the memory of some old people now living.' Here, as usual, Dr. Reeves' information is strictly accurate, although at the present day the site of the chapel appears, as such, to be forgotten by the natives. Upon the rough promontory of Ceann Fasachd,[1] about a quarter of a mile west from Traigh Ghortain, and at a somewhat greater distance north of Carn a' Bhraighe, are the remains of a rectangular enclosure, divided by an east and west wall through its centre. Within the southern half, with walls now about 3 feet high, are the ruins of the chapel, rounded exteriorly to the east, but square on the west, and the interior squared throughout. A curious feature is an 8-foot wide causeway leading from the chapel into the northern half of the enclosure, and there expanding in an outward curve at both sides.

+VI

'At Clappach, in the middle of the island, there was a chapel and burying-ground.' This must refer to CLABHACH,[2] between

---

[1] *Fasachd* is the spelling upon the Ordnance map. It is Gaelic for 'desolateness.' *Fasach* similarly means 'a desert.'

[2] This chapel would seem to have been dedicated to St. Kenneth, as 'Kilchainie' is marked upon a map in *Origines Parochiales* (vol. ii. part i.), close to the shore about midway between Grishipol and Cliad. Blaeu's Atlas of 1662 places the same name a little farther to the north.

Ballyhogh and Grishipol, which may be said to be in the middle
of Coll (as regards length), although close to its west shore.
Here is the present Established Church, between which and
the sea, upon a mound to the north of Clabhach Burn, just
above Traigh Grianaig,[1] may be the remains of this graveyard.
Upon one small upright stone is painted 'In memory of Dido,'
said to commemorate a dog or cat! But perhaps the incongruity
need not at all detract from the probability of this having
really been a Christian burial-place, although no signs of any
chapel could be traced.

'At GALLANACH, also near the middle of the island, was   +VII
a chapel and burying-ground.' These seem to have been upon
a small green mound about 300 yards north-west of Arinabost,
and within two miles from Clabhach. Local tradition agrees
as to the site.

'At Kilfinnaig is a cemetery, which is still used, and where
there was formerly a chapel.' This is, of course, KILLUNAIG,[2]   +VIII
close to the Bousd road-track, and a mile north of Arinabost,
being the second of the, two burial-grounds at present in use.
The chapel still remains, measuring some 33 by 16 feet, and
the walls about 6 feet high inside, although much silted up by
sand without. Possibly, in Dr. Reeves' time the whole chapel
may have been thus covered. A native of Coll tells how his
grandfather remembered boys climbing up the eastern gable to
a window there, and that a bell hung above. Both window

---

[1] Thus locally, but upon the Ordnance Survey 'Bagh Craimneach.'
[2] In *Origines Parochiales* the dedication of this chapel is attributed to St. Senaic.

and bell are now absent, the latter taken, it is said, by a farm-servant at midnight, as a piece of bravado, to the house at Gallanach, where it was afterwards used to summon the labourers home to dinner! This was a burial-place of the MacLeans—indeed exclusively so, according to tradition—and certainly all the older stones which bear either arms or inscriptions have belonged to that clan. There are nine or ten large flat slabs within the graveyard, at least one of them being of the West Highland or Iona type.

+ IX   'At ARINTLUICH, on the S.E. of the island, was a chapel and cemetery.' This place is unmarked upon the six-inch Ordnance Survey, though Arintluichd [1] is locally known and pointed out near Fiskary, fully a mile south of Arinagour. No burial-ground is there remembered; but nearly a mile south of Fiskary, upon the point immediately to the north of a large shallow bay called Port an Eathair, are the remains of a causeway (or of close stepping-stones) leading out to a small rocky plateau, where has been some building, not improbably the missing chapel. There have been numerous crofts between Fiskary and Port an Eathair.

+ X   'At KILBRIDE, S.E. of Gallanach, was a chapel and cemetery.' This is a misleading description of Kilbride, which is about two miles south-west of Arinagour, close to Acha, and near the east or opposite shore from Gallanach, being distant thence at least four miles due south. This burying-ground is about a quarter of a mile south of the present Kilbride farmhouse, but close

---

[1] 'The shieling of the hollow.'

to the west of the site of a former one. It is flat and rather spacious, of somewhat circular shape, and has been several times under tillage; remains of its enclosing wall still show, but there are practically no traces of the chapel.

'At Greamsary was a chapel and cemetery, called BEARRIGREIN +XI At Totamore, near the west side of Coll, about 500 yards north of Grimisary and just above the north-east edge of an extensive meadow known as Machair Mor (half way between Loch nan Cinneachan and Hogh Bay), is a large irregular—and yet somewhat rectangular—enclosure which is this Bearrigrein.[1] Near its north-west corner are the ruins of a cottage, and behind it was the graveyard, which however, having been under cultivation for many years, shows no distinctive traces, except a very few bones which may be human.

There is also said to have been a burial-ground to the west of Loch Ronard, towards the north end of Coll, but of this no trace could be seen.

About 300 yards east from the mission-house, upon the opposite side of Loch Eatharna, just where the stream enters the sea-loch, is a bracken-covered mound, which seems to be an ancient site of some description, although its precise character has not been satisfactorily determined. Immediately south of this mound, upon the flat ground close to the mouth of the

---

[1] In the island of Boreray (off North Uist, and formerly possessed by a MacLean of Coll) is another 'Barradh greine'; the translation being 'a place facing the sun,' very applicable to the Bearrigrein in Coll.

burn, are the remains of several rectangular buildings, all formed of massive stones, very much larger than are to be seen in any other of the remains in Coll. One of these erections stands about east and west, and another, composed of really huge blocks of stone, north and south, with an interior of 15 by 12 feet. It is just possible that one of these may have been a Christian chapel, as no remains of any pre-Reformation place of worship are known elsewhere within at least two miles from Arinagour, the port and only existing village of Coll.

CHAPTER VII

COLL—ITS CLAN HISTORY

In addition to those antiquities of Coll which have already been described, there are, upon the shore of Loch Breacacha, the ruins of an old castle of the MacLeans. The main building, a massive keep, is of mediæval date, and may well have been erected about the time when the island of Coll (with other lands) was granted by King Robert the Bruce to Angus Oig, or when, a little later (12th June 1343), it was included in a charter from David II. to John, Lord of the Isles. The keep itself has been of five stories, with walls 7 ft. 6 in. thick, a width sufficient to contain several small separate chambers, of which one at least is yet to be seen complete. From the south-east angle of the hall upon the first floor (or second story) rises a corkscrew staircase, now much broken, access to which is given by a doorway with dog-tooth ornament carved upon its lintel. The cement used in the oldest portion of the castle is coarse though very tenacious, chiefly composed of shells; it was curious to find some fragments of slate imbedded in the mortar of the keep, apparently debris from an earlier structure, at a break in the wall immediately beneath the small chamber to which reference has just been made. The keep has received additions in the way of outer buildings at evidently two distinct later periods. This old Breacacha Castle has been disused since about the year 1750, when the modern castle was erected a hundred and fifty yards to the north, and it was in this latter residence that Dr. Johnson was entertained by the laird of Coll in the autumn of 1773.

Grishipol House, where Dr. Johnson also spent one night, is close to the west shore of the island, and its construction and style appear to give it a date of about the latter half of the seventeenth century. The masonry is still tolerably complete, with the exception that the south-west corner is now in a dangerous condition, having had many of its stones pulled out near the base comparatively recently, in search, it is said, for golden treasure. It is not a large house, being a simple oblong of two stories with attics, and the timbers which form the lintels of the windows and interior doorways are most plainly made from wreckage.

According to credible tradition there seems however to have been an earlier dwelling—probably fortified—upon or near the same site, erected by Fionnaghal (widow of Lachlan Bronnach,[1] seventh chief of MacLean, and daughter of William MacLeod of Harris), after her second marriage, with Gilleonan MacNeil of Barra. By her first husband, Lachlan Bronnach, she had two sons, one of whom, John Garbh, apparently born about 1450, demanded an inheritance from the Lord of the Isles, and received the island of Coll in addition to lands in Mull. John Garbh thus became the

---

[1] He was alive in 1463, and Fionnaghal was his second wife. Lachlan Oig, only son by his first marriage, succeeded as eighth chief of Clan MacLean.

BREACACHA CASTLE.

first MacLean of Coll, although his grandfather Hector, sixth chief of MacLean (slain at Harlaw in 1411), had held at least a portion of that island—*terras 6 marcarum de Tyrvnghafeal*[1]— as vassal under Donald, second Lord of the Isles, by a charter dated Ardtornish, 1st November 1409 ; while Lachlan Lubanach, fifth chief of MacLean, who married a daughter of John, first Lord of the Isles, had possessed all Tiree under a similar charter of date 12th July 1390. The story runs that MacNeil of Barra assumed possession of his young stepson's property of Coll, and occupied Breacacha Castle. John Garbh therefore retired to Ireland for several years, but upon some fresh provocation returned with a few armed followers and landed in Coll with a band of fifty men, there to learn that his stepfather ' with six score men ' was engaged in building a house at Grishipol.[2] Local tradition says that John Garbh was afraid to challenge so large a company, and passed by Grishipol towards the north, being then thought by MacNeil to have

[1] *Reg. Mag. Sig.*, 1495, a confirmation of the original charter of 1409. Tyrvnghafeal has been somewhat difficult to identify through its disguise of *Tyrvughafeal* in *Reg. Mag. Sig.*, but certainly represents ' Tirunga Foill ' (*Fealda* in *Reg. Mag. Sig.* of 1528 and 1542), the first half of the word denoting a measurement of land corresponding with *unciata* (see Skene's *Celtic Scotland*, second edition, vol. iii. p. 403. Captain Thomas in *Proc. Soc. Antiq. Scot.*, vol. xx. pp. 200-213, proves the Pictish *davach*, the Gaelic *tir-unga*, and the Norse *unciata*, to be synonymous). *Teringa de Killis* (Caoles in Coll) appears in the *Retours* (Argyllshire, No. 93, 1695), and *Tyrungachornage* (Cornaig, also in Coll), in *Origines Parochiales*, vol. ii. p. 834.

[2] *A History of the Clan MacLean*, by J. P. MacLean, Cincinnati, 1889. This, together with *An Historical and Genealogical Account of the Clan MacLean*, by ' a Seneachie,' London, 1838, and Gregory's *History of the Western Highlands and Isles of Scotland*, Edinburgh, 1836, have been largely drawn upon as to the genealogy of the Clan MacLean.

retreated.   Immediately afterwards, however, the MacLeans, feeling ashamed of making no effort to recover their own property, summoned fresh courage and turned sharply to the west through a narrow pass in the rocks which is still pointed out, while MacNeil followed them northwards, and the MacLeans by this detour coming upon Grishipol House, were able to seize it in its undefended state.   Other accounts describe a tough fight at Grishipol upon this occasion, and give details of a hand-to-hand combat between one of John Garbh's supporters (a Campbell) and MacNeil's body-servant, in the course of which, Campbell, to avoid a stroke, made a gigantic leap backwards (or sideways) and upwards across the stream near the ruins of the present old Grishipol mansion-house—the exact spot being still shown.   It is added that MacLean and his company were hard pressed and driven to the beach, where, making a stand, they drove their opponents down the shore, and there, in a small bay just to the north of Grishipol point, slew Gilleonan MacNeil with many of his followers.

According to this chronology the fight at Grishipol must have taken place between about 1470 and 1480, but the greatest difficulties are found in the endeavour to make history and tradition agree, an attempt which is perhaps futile, even while admitting that local tradition usually holds a certain substratum of distorted history.

Another story tells of a similar encounter between the MacLeans and the MacNeils upon the beach opposite Eilean Ornsay in the east of Coll, and, as has already been mentioned, the

MacNeils seem to have also sustained a severe defeat on the island of Gunna.

The battle at Sruthan nan Ceann, near Totronald, is said to have been fought in 1596 between Sir Lachlan Mor (fourteenth chief of MacLean) and Lachlan, sixth MacLean of Coll,[1] immediately upon the latter's attainment of his majority, when the interlopers were defeated with great slaughter, although shortly afterwards, upon the landing of a larger force, the victory was reversed.

It is worthy of note that in the *Acts of Parliament of Scotland*, 1587, in a list of 'landislordis and baillies of landis . . . . . quhair brokin men hes duelt and presentlie duellis,' is included 'the Laird of Coll,' so that it seems neither impossible nor improbable that some of the more remote Duns may have been inhabited by these outlaws of only three hundred years ago.

It was not indeed until the year 1609 — through 'The Band and Statutes of Icolmkill' — that the autocratic clan-system began to be finally broken down and the authority of the King of Scotland nominally established in the Hebrides; although up to the years 1645-1647 practically the whole population of Coll and Tiree is described as being 'in actuall rebellioun.'[2]

In a report drawn up sometime between the years 1577 and 1595 (probably about 1590) Coll is said to be 'very fertile alsweill

---

[1] MacLean's *History of the Clan MacLean*, pp. 125, 285.
[2] See note as to 'The Band and Statutes of Icolmkill' in Chapter xv.

of corns as of all kind of catell. Thair is sum little birkin woodis within the said Ile.'[1] Birch, together with all other natural wood, is now entirely absent, if a few small trees at Breacacha Gardens and some scrubby undergrowth upon one or two small islands be left out of account.

[1] Skene's *Celtic Scotland*, second edition, vol. iii. p. 437. It appears that Iona contained thickets or brushwood in St. Columba's time (' *in saltibus*,' Reeves' *Adamnan*, p. 205).

CHAPTER VIII

THE TRESHNISH ISLES

SOME notice may be included of this group of islands, which however belongs to Mull, forming part of the united parish of Kilninian and Kilmore. The Treshnish Isles[1] (six or more in number, according as the smaller are reckoned) lie eight to ten miles south-east from Coll, but much nearer to the west coast of Mull. They are here described on account of the existence upon them of at least one Dun or Rock-Fort (of peculiar type), and two fortresses, doubtless of a distinctly later or mediæval period.[2] These more modern forts are upon the northmost pair of islands —Cairn a' Burgh Beg and Cairn a' Burgh Mor—separated by a narrow channel, one (or both) of these falling to be identified

[1] The present writer has visited all the six larger islets of this group, which comprises the far-famed island of Staffa, so interesting from a geological point of view, but as this last-named does not seem to bear any traces of ancient occupation, no description of it is here attempted.

[2] According to one tradition the Cairnburgs formed the boundary-line between the northern and southern governments of the Hebrides or Sudreys, when these were subject to the Norwegian kings. Another account states Ardnamurchan Point to have been the dividing-line. It may be incidentally noted that (A.D. 560-574) two hundred years before the main Viking immigration, Iona and the adjacent islands seem to have been a debatable ground between the Scots or Dalriads on the south and the Picts to the north—both of these nations (or branches of the same nation) having a joint interest in Iona, and each of them giving a separate grant of it to St. Columba about the year 560 (Skene's *Celtic Scotland*, second edition, vol. ii. p. 87). The *Nordureyer* was applied to the Orkneys, as distinguished from the *Sudureyer* or entire Hebrides (*Ibid.*, vol. i. p. 495).

with the strong castle of Kernaborg or Cairnburg,[1] which the Lord of Lorn, when yielding Mull and other lands to the Lord of the Isles in 1354, stipulated not to be given into keeping of any of the race of Clan Finnon (MacKinnon).[2]

Lachlan Lubanach (fifth chief of MacLean) had from Donald of the Isles, 12th July 1390, two charters, the first conveying the custody and constableship of Duart and other castles, and the second giving 'the keepership of the castles of Kernaborg and Isleborg, with the small (? islands) Floda and Lunga,' etc.[3]—Fladda and Lunga being others of the Treshnish group.[4]   Hector Odhar (ninth chief of MacLean, and fourth in direct descent from Lachlan Lubanach) commanded the fleet of the Lord of the Isles at the clan battle of Bloody Bay in 1482, off the north end of Mull, and was there taken prisoner.[5]   Until his forfeiture in 1493 he was

---

[1] According to *Origines Parochiales*, vol. ii. p. 322, 'Kiarnaborg, the Bjana or Bjarnar-borg of the Sagas.' In 1249, Kiarnaborg, together with three other castles in the Hebrides, was held by John 'King of the Isles,' under King Haco of Norway (*Haco's Expedition* ; see also the '*Rolls*' (*Icelandic Sagas*), vol. ii. p. 260—Hakonar Saga, *anno* 1248).   The castle of 'Scraburgh' mentioned in the *Exchequer Rolls*, vol. i. p. 238 (*anno* 1329), is supposed to be Cairnburg.   After all, 'Scraburgh' and 'Cairnburg' are practically synonymous, seeming to mean respectively 'notched-fort' in Norse (*cf.* the Cumbrian 'scarf' for mountain-pass) and 'rock-fort' in Gaelic.   'Skarfr-borg,' or 'cormorant-fort,' would again be equally descriptive. In Thomson's *Acts of the Parliament of Scotland*, vol. xii. p. 6, under date 12th June 1343, David II. granted to John (Lord) of the Isles, several of the Hebrides, including 'insulam de Mule cum suis minutis insulis, insulas de Tiryad et de Colla, cum suis minutis insulis,' etc. ; together with 'custodias castrorum nostrorum de Kernoborgh, Iselborgh, et Dunchonall, cum terris et minutis insulis ad dicta castra pertinentibus.'

[2] Gregory, p. 80.

[3] *Reg. Mag. Sig.*, 1495, confirming the charter of 1390—'constabulariam et custodiam castrorum de Kernaborg et Isleborg, unacum minutis Floda et Lunga,' etc.

[4] Dun Cruit upon a rock off Lunga will be noticed later.

[5] Gregory, p. 69.

CAIRNBURG BEG, FROM SOUTH.

CAIRNBURG MOR, FROM NORTH.

WALLS ON CAIRNBURG MOR, FROM NORTH.

ENTRANCE TO CAIRNBURG MOR, FROM NORTH.

heritable keeper of 'Carneburg,' Isleborg, and three other castles in the Sudreys; he fell at Flodden in 1513.

Cairnburg Castle was evidently besieged by the royal forces about the year 1505, warlike stores for this purpose (including artillery and 'gun-stanes' or stone bullets) being dispatched from Dumbarton in 1504;[1] but again, some ten years later, 1513-1514, it was retaken by Lachlan Catanach MacLean of Duart.[2]

From a passing reference in a contract between the Bishop of the Isles and MacLean of Duart in 1580, when provision was made for eight men to keep the fortress of Cairnburg during the absence of the last-named upon military service under the King of Scotland, it would appear that MacLean had up to that date held it under his special care, if indeed he did not make it his residence.[3]

Even so late as the rebellion of 1715 Cairnburg was garrisoned

---

[1] Gregory, pp. 100-101.

[2] *Ibid.*, p. 115.

[3] *Collectanea de Rebus Albanicis*, p. 16. In Thomson's *Acts of the Parliament of Scotland*, vol. vi. part ii. pp. 167-168 (*anno* 1649), reference is made—upon the supplication of Hector MacLean of Torloisk—to the facts that Lieutenant-General David Leslie 'in anno 1647 having gotten the Delyverance of the strengths and houses belonging to the Makleans, Hee then intrusted to the said Hector the hous and strength of Cairnbolg, quhilk sensyne hee hes faithfullie keeped with threttie men in garrison upon his owne charges for the vse of the publict now be the space of eightene monethes, . . . And that the said Hector was for a long tyme in sommer last bloked up in a maner within the said strength be Sr. Lauchlane McLeane for not rendering theirof.' In response, 'parlement Considering the necessity of keeping the said strength of Carnbolg for the use of the publict in tyme comeing, Haue appointed the said Hector To be Captan and Keeper theirof and allowes to him a Lieutennent a serjant Tuo corporallis a drummer and threttie souldioris To be payed according to the pay of the kingdome.' Hector (second MacLean of Torloisk) and Sir Lachlan MacLean (first baronet of Morvern and of Duart) were first cousins. The eldest son of the latter was 'the heroic Hector Roy,' killed at the battle of Inverkeithing in July 1651.

by the MacLeans, and was taken and recaptured more than once.[1]

Of the two Cairnburgs, the nearer to Mull is Cairnburg Beg, which includes a high rocky plateau to the north-east, measuring fully two hundred yards in each direction and isolated on all sides by precipitous cliffs, quite inaccessible except to the south-west from a comparatively level space of somewhat equal area, whence the entrance has been by a steep slanting pathway. The lower section is bounded upon the south by rough rocks at the seashore, and has been protected both to east and west by thick walls, of which considerable portions remain. Within these walls appears to have been one circular building in a central position, together with at least three others (perhaps of rectangular shape) near the base of the fort itself. Upon the north-western edge of the elevated plateau are traces of a dry-stone wall, and at this point occur small fragments of rude pottery of the Dun type; while all along the southern (or entrance) side there still remains a distinct, although by no means substantial, stone and lime fortification about four feet high, pierced at intervals by narrow loop-holes. Immediately above the steep approach is a kitchen-midden, containing bones, with many limpet and oyster shells. Upon the south wall of Cairnburg Beg grows a fine ivy, apparently not indigenous, although the same is found upon the north-east wall of Cairnburg Mor, and also occurs upon the rocks on the east of Fladda.

Cairnburg Mor is a larger island close to the south-west of Cairnburg Beg, and has no low-lying portion. Its north-east and

[1] *New Stat. Acc.*, vol. vii. p. 342 ; the reference being clearly to Cairnburg Mor.

only practicable side is lined by a similar wall to that upon Cairnburg Beg, with the addition that in parts (notably one, where it is very lofty, with two loop-holes above) the artificial protection, on account of the natural weakness of the cliff, has been made much deeper. There appear to have been three accesses, all from the north-east. The main entrance is much the larger and more elaborate, and is farthest north. Here, across a wide gully, is an exterior dry-stone dyke, and then a second of the same character, but diagonal. Within comes a stone and lime wall, beyond which is, a little below the summit, a small plateau, guarded by this eastern wall of stone and lime, and upon the west by another and still higher one. Immediately to the south of this approach, upon the large level summit, is a rectangular and comparatively modern building of stone and lime standing nearly east and west, with rafter-holes in its west gable, the doorway (45 inches wide and slightly splayed) being to the north. To the south are the remains of a small independent erection, of interior dimensions 26 by 16 feet; the fact that against its east end is an oblong built table (57 by 39 inches, and three feet above the present base) rendering it probable that this was a *chapel*. The floor is partly composed of bare rock, and in the east gable (north of the altar, if altar it be) is a small bole or cupboard, all in keeping with its suggested character. The thickness of the walls is about 26 inches.

Some thirty yards south from this supposed chapel is a third rectangular house, without gables but containing curious vertical recesses in the interior walls, in which have evidently stood

upright timbers supporting the roof from all four sides. This
dwelling (which does not appear to be even of mediæval date,
and bears no signs of fortification) consists of two rooms, measuring inside about 29 feet by 15½ feet and 16 feet 3 inches by
15 feet 9 inches respectively, the larger one, at least, having had
an upper story, of which some windows are clearly traceable.
In the larger room are nine, and in the smaller five, of the vertical
recesses in the walls.

The main entrance to the fort has already been described, but
farther east have been evidently two others, each with a guard-
room at the top. The first is very well marked, and has a flat-
arched doorway, through a narrow gully. The second is ruder
and more difficult of access.

Fladda is a heather-covered island nearly a mile long, and
towards its south end is a low-lying grassy isthmus, with a natural
harbour upon each side. In the centre of this level are the foundations of a wide circular wall, which seems the more significant from
the fact that quite near it are six small mounds of turf and
stones. If there was any Dun on Fladda this seems to be the site.
Fladda lies to the south of the two Cairnburgs, and further
southward is Lunga, much the largest of the Treshnish Isles,
being a mile and a half in length. The only object of antiquity
of any importance at Lunga is Dun Cruit,[1] a rugged and
isolated rock off the west shore, so precipitous as to be—at the
present day at least—entirely inaccessible. Upon this high rock
are the remains of walls distinctly traceable, so that, apart from

[1] Meaning 'Pictish fort.' This is a most peculiar and even significant name.

DUN CRUIT, FROM SOUTH-EAST.

DUN CRUIT, FROM SOUTH (DISTANT).

DUN CRUIT, FROM NORTH-EAST.

BAC MOR, from south.

its name, it seems to be a veritable Dun.   When so occupied, the probability (if not certainty) is that the approach was by means of a drawbridge across the narrow 'sloc,' or precipitous gully to the east, as is afterwards suggested in connection with the somewhat parallel case of 'An Dunan' upon Eilean Dubh in Tiree. Such is indeed said also to have been the latest attempted mode of access, when a man lost his life through the breaking of a mast over which he tried to drag himself.   The rock is now tenanted by a vast colony of puffins, which (in the nesting season at least) continually march forwards in detachments, flying off as they reach the brink of the precipice.

About three miles south-west of Lunga is another of the Treshnish group—a double island indeed, consisting of Bac Mor ('The Dutchman's Cap') and Bac Beg.   Upon its east shoulder, below the prominent 'Cap,' are the ruins of three small circular erections—probably old shielings.   Bac Mor is about half a mile long and is now tenanted only by Highland cattle, as to which a local saying runs that nineteen will thrive upon this island, but twenty would starve—surely a most precise computation !

CHAPTER IX

TIREE—GENERAL

THE Island of Tiree[1] lies only two miles south-west of Coll, with a length of twelve miles and an average breadth of three, though the latter varies between one and six miles, so irregular is the outline of its shores. Coll and Tiree are much alike in area, and equally prolific in ancient sites of forts and chapels, but here the resemblance ends, and whether regard be had to the various aspects of topographical configuration, general fertility, the present condition of their antiquities, or the actual number of population, a decided contrast is most apparent.

The main portion of Tiree is quite flat, interrupted however by six distinct hills which look all the higher in comparison. Three of these, by far the larger both in base and height, are towards the south end of the island, viz., Ben Hogh, Ben Kenavara, and Ben Hynish, the latter of 460 feet; while in the middle and northern parts are other three lower isolated hills, —Ben Gott, Ben Balaphetrish, and Dun Mor a' Chaolais, all of comparatively slight elevation, and each crowned by a Dun.

With a similar area to that of Coll, Tiree has five times the population, the exact figures being ·2192 at the census of 1901, as

---

[1] 'Tiry' in the old *Stat. Acc.*, and often yet spelt 'Tyree.'

SCARINISH, FROM EAST.

KELP-BURNING, KENAVARA.

against 432 in Coll. Even this is a considerable reduction since 1881, when the number of souls in Tiree was 2730, while the old *Stat. Acc.* gives 2416 and 1509 for the years 1792 and 1755 respectively.[1] These facts are not surprising when one considers that a very large proportion of Tiree being arable, crofters and cottars are thickly scattered in groups or 'townships' throughout the whole island. The name of Tiree is supposed to mean 'the land of corn,' and certainly at the present day it is a land of crofters.

With these statistics in view, it seems quite contradictory to find that, upon the whole, the Duns of Tiree are in much better preservation than those of the neighbouring island of Coll, even although there is room for regret that fresh dilapidations have evidently occurred within very recent years. In regard to the condition of the ancient chapels, there is not so much to choose between the two islands, and the generally superior state of the Tiree Duns is doubtless chiefly attributable to the existence among them of a well-defined and more massive type which we have described in Class A as semi-Brochs. This class is apparently quite absent in Coll, where the Duns are mostly rude Hill-Forts, simply following the outline of the rocks upon which they are built, or small Islet-Forts, a type which is comparatively rare in Tiree.

It is noteworthy that in Tiree (as in others of the Hebridean

[1] The kelp industry, at the commencement of the last century, gave a great impetus to the population, which by the time of the potato failure in 1846 had reached over 5000, to be reduced again to 3706 in the year 1851. Owing to new chemical methods, the entire abandonment of kelp-burning in Tiree is now (1902) contemplated.

islands) occasional survivals of the cruder and now generally obsolete forms of domestic appliances are still to be met with, although these are fast dying out and may soon be practically non-existent.

A few specimens of unglazed pottery (or 'craggans,' Gaelic *crogan*), closely resembling the Dun type, are yet to be found— globular-shaped jars varying considerably in size; and indeed the last local maker of the small urn-like cups (Flora Brown of Sandaig) died so recently as the spring of 1896. Even within late years these small craggans (made of clay from Balaphuil, near the south end of Tiree) were in request for cases of consumptive disease; the vessel was first heated upon the fire, and milk being drawn into it from the cow, the doubly-warm draught was administered to the patient with an effect which was supposed to be peculiarly beneficial.

In 1897 at least two hand-querns were to be seen, although without the necessary wooden fittings, and natives of not more than middle age remember their being in regular use throughout the island. [1]

There is said to be still upon a door at Kilmoluag a quaint lock and key entirely composed of wood, and the writer possesses a model made from another of similar type. In the barn of Hynish farm, and in actual use, are five rather curious wooden bolts, each running through three brackets of the same material, two of these brackets being upon the door and the third upon the jamb as a slot. These fastenings seem to be of quite recent

[1] The old *Stat. Acc.*, vol. x. p. 399, states of Tiree (*anno* 1794) that 'the work of 50 women is yearly lost at grinding' by these querns or hand-mills.

OLD CRAGGAN, ACTUAL SIZE.

FANNING-HUT AT CAOLES.

make, and the shape of the bolt bears a distinct resemblance to that of the wooden lock just mentioned.

At Acarseid an Duin, Caoles, upon a very short burnlet which rises in Loch a' Mhuilinn (now a mere marsh in summer-time), are the scanty remains of a rude corn-mill; but except for slight traces of its walls and of the mill-lade, the site is very indistinct. Near it, until three or four years ago, stood a fanning-house of comparatively modern erection—a small hut (since ruined) roofed with turf upon bare rafters, its door towards the north and in the opposite side a small window as also a square opening upon the floor-level. Mr. Hugh MacDonald (postmaster of Tiree, and a native of Caoles) states that this fanning-house had formerly doors in its four sides so as to catch all winds, and also that his ancestors had been millers in Caoles ever since the year 1725. He describes the mill as of ' Norwegian' type, and adds that it was in operation until about 1885. Mr. M'Diarmid, factor to the Duke of Argyll, also remembers the mill at work within the past twenty years.

The fanning-hut, when we visited it in 1899 and found it in fair order, was occupied by a disused loom, close to which lay a curved (almost serpentine) shuttle and another wooden implement (toothed like the head of a large rake) used in connection with the loom—presumably as a ' reed.' [1]

---

[1] In 1899 there were in Tiree less than a dozen looms in use, and these generally by old people who weave into cloth for the crofters yarns supplied by them. Each of the townships of Scarinish, Vaul, Cornaig, Balaphuil, and Mannel then possessed at least one loom. At Mannel the writer had an opportunity of seeing a loom at work, the shuttle being passed through the 'shed' *by hand*, without the appliance of any mechanical striker.

Between this hut and the shore (which is quite close to it) a bridge crosses the lade, its span consisting of a fine mill-stone four feet in diameter. This stone was brought from Coll and formed the lower of the two in Caoles mill. The upper is now in two halves, one fragment supporting this bridge, the other serving as the flagstone in front of Mr. MacDonald's cottage. The pair previously in use at Caoles (replaced by the above) were smaller, and are not now to be seen.

CHAPTER X

TIREE—DUNS, OR ANCIENT FORTS

CLASS A

THE SEMI-BROCH TYPE [1]

IT may be bold to introduce a new name in our description of the Tiree Duns, but a type seems to occur here which is not only distinct from the ruder Hill-Forts, but apparently also from the true Brochs (or so-called Pictish Towers) of the northern counties of Scotland, and of the Orkneys and Shetlands. [2]

This class consists of substantial circular or sub-circular dry-stone erections enclosing a central space some 35 to 40 feet in diameter. The wall, which now never exceeds about six feet in height, has within its thickness a passage or ground gallery, more or less continuous, and varying from 28 to 36

---

[1] These, in their double walls, bear some resemblance to the Irish Cashels, which, however, are very much larger in area, and seem in some cases to have been built for the protection of cattle. In Scotland there is at least one example of the cashel type in Glenmore, Glenelg; this is an irregular oval enclosure measuring some 20 by 30 yards, and is known as 'Na Bathaichean,' Gaelic for 'the cow-houses.'

[2] See also Chapter xv. upon 'Characteristics of the Duns and Sandhill-sites of Coll and Tiree.' The Brochs nearest in geographical situation are a scattered group in Glenelg, and a fine single specimen at Carloway, Lewis.

inches wide.   Even the best-preserved show no traces of a
stair or of upper galleries between the double walls, and therefore seem to have been of only one story.   In this respect
the semi-Broch type differs essentially from that of the Broch
proper, although otherwise somewhat approximating to it.   We
accordingly hazard the suggestion that Class A may form a
link between these two very distinct styles of Dun—the
Broch and the simple Rock-Fort. [1]

In each of the four clearly-defined semi-Brochs of Tiree, the
main fort is supplemented by two or more separate outer
defensive walls, a point in which they resemble a good many
Brochs, although others seem to have had no outworks whatever.   Further, the two or three better preserved contain,
within their central courtyard, traces of small round or oval
cells, although it is now difficult to judge whether or not these
may be the remains of a secondary occupation.   The present
writer inclines to the belief that they formed part of the
original plan, and this mainly because of their special (if
slender) association with Class A (as apart from Class B) and
their thorough adaptation and regular positions.

Commencing near the north end of Tiree, the first of this type

[1] The affinity to the Brochs consists in the massive circular form, with a clear passage
between the main walls, although indeed this passage in scarcely any case seems to have
been quite continuous, disappearing downwards, with a dipping roof, at Dun Mor a' Chaolais
and Dun Mor Vaul, and being obstructed by massive rock at Dun Hiader.

A perusal of Captain Thomas's paper 'On the Duns of the Outer Hebrides' (*Archæologia
Scotica*, vol. v., 1890) suggests that several of the Duns enumerated by him in the Long
Island (notably at pp. 373, 382, 404) approach the semi-Broch type, as possessing cells or
ground galleries between the main walls, and yet not being true Brochs.

SEMI-BROCHS,—DUN MOR A' CHAOLAIS, from south.

SEMI-BROCHS,—DUN MOR VAUL, FROM SOUTH.

is to be found upon the crest of the hill (128 feet) named after the fort, DUN MOR A' CHAOLAIS.[1]

●1

Here remain portions of several concentric walls, especially towards the south-east of the summit; while to the south, some 15 yards beyond the outer rampart, are the foundations of a small isolated round erection, only 9 feet across.

The interior of the main Dun measures about 39 feet in diameter, enclosed by double walls (12 or 13 feet over both), of which the outer is about 6 and the inner fully 4 feet in thickness, with evidence, at several points, of a narrow passage or ground gallery between them. The roof of this clearly dips downwards towards the east, the passage itself being there 36 inches wide, while at the opposite or west side it can be traced on a higher level, and may thus have been continuous throughout the whole circuit, or nearly so, as in the case of other well-marked Duns of this type. The external diameter of the main fort is thus some 60 to 65 feet, and then comes an exterior wall at a distance of about 6 feet, with still farther out another (or third) defence at a varying distance extending so far as 11 yards on the south, where at least two courses of very large stones still remain *in situ*.

The surface of the inner Dun is completely strewn with large stones, and if any interior constructions existed—notably towards

[1] Upon the small map of Tiree which accompanies Dr. Reeves' valuable monograph (already mentioned in Chapter vi.) the narrow bay immediately to the east of this fort, now termed Acarseid an Duin, or 'anchorage of the Dun,' is marked 'Downkifil Harbour.' This place-name could not be verified, but it raises the question whether possibly Dun Mor a' Chaolais may have originally been known as *Dun Kifil* or some phonetic equivalent.

the east—the mass of debris greatly obscures their identification. Altogether this has been a massive fort, of considerable strength and importance, and the two Duns—Mor and Beg—at Vaul are within clear view. Very few relics were observed, these indeed being confined to a few fragments of pottery, including a single patterned piece. We are informed that the Rev. J. G. Campbell[1] used to dig here, and that he found 'buttons' of baked clay—otherwise, earthenware whorls.[2] In a field a few hundred yards to the west a fine hammer-stone was picked up, near the end of a narrow causeway which runs in a northerly direction up a steep rugged bank south of Dun Mor a' Chaolais, having perhaps been a church-path between Sgibinis and the former chapel of Crois a' Chaolais, about a mile distant.

Upon the other side of the island, at a distance of three miles and just above the rocky shore to the west of Vaul Bay, is DUN MOR VAUL,[3] the most distinct specimen in Tiree of the semi-Broch type, all the better defined because of its partial excavation some twenty years ago by the present Duke of Argyll (then Marquis of Lorne).

The inner or main fort, with its double concentric walls (28 to 36 inches apart, and enclosing an area about 35 feet in

---

[1] For many years parish minister of Tiree. He died in November 1891.

[2] A stone whorl—found in Mr. Campbell's time, if not by him—was shown to us. It measures an inch and three-quarters in diameter, and is pierced by a quarter-inch hole. See Dunan Nighean, *postea*, as to pottery whorls.

[3] A name evidently of Norse origin; whether as 'Walls' in Orkney and Shetland from the same root as 'voe' (*vágr*, a bay), or from *völlr*, a field (*vellir* = fields, *valla* = of fields).

diameter) is strongly built of very large stones, six courses remaining in position on the north exterior.[1]

The outer wall is about 6 feet thick, the inner varying from 3 to 4 feet, giving a diameter of some 60 feet across the walls, a measurement which closely corresponds with that of the other Duns of this class. At the south-east the yard-wide interval or ground-gallery between the walls has been cleared to a depth of about 4 feet, sufficiently to show its character most distinctly. It disappears where the roof slopes downwards at the east, reappearing a few yards farther on, but merely to disappear again (unless this be a cell within the walls) and recommences towards the north, about 8 or 10 yards from its first dip, thence extending continuously round the remainder of the wall.

The cleared portion of the gallery between the double walls runs from south to north-east, and near its beginning—that is, at mid-south—is a small bit of its roof still remaining *in situ*, consisting of two long stones placed across it upon others which project underneath from either side. Towards the north, similar projections partly cross the upper part of the passage or gallery, but without any existent cap-stones. The centre space of the Dun is completely and thickly strewn with loose stones of a good size, and contains (evidently above the level of the original floor) one cell 42 inches in diameter, while there are traces of three or four others.

Outside, surrounding the double-walled fort, is an exterior

---

[1] In the summer of 1901 this wall was unfortunately much deteriorated from its condition so recently as 1897, when our photograph was taken.

rampart which follows the summit of the rock on the west and north, at a greatly varying distance—44 feet beyond the inner fort to the north, 26 feet to the south, and only 12 to 15 feet on the west, where the rocks fall abruptly. Within the large space to the north and a smaller one to the north-west are the foundations of five or six small round or oval erections, now showing as hollows of about 6 by 8 feet, having evidently been rude huts, between which and the main Dun the natural rock crops out in massive form.   Still farther out, extending from mid-south to the north-east is a fourth wall to cover the approach and enclose a small well on the south, marked upon the Ordnance map as 'Tobar Duin Mhoir.'

Not much was found here—merely broken hammer-stones and small round pebbles similar to those already noticed in Coll, with a very little pottery (including a few fragments with raised or indented patterns), two flints, and a flat round slaty stone which may have been the cover of a craggan.   This Dun is within sight of that at Balaphetrish.

The next fort which seems to be of the same general design is DUN BORAIGE MOR,[1] a quarter of a mile west from the south end of Traigh Bail' a' Mhuilinn.   Its ruins show that it must have been most substantial in structure, covering, with its dependencies, a very large area, in this respect coming next in extent to Dun na Cleite, to be afterwards noticed.   The boundary fence of Hogh farm runs right across the centre of the Dun, and

---

[1] Boraige appears to be merely a corruption of the Norse *Borg* (or Broch), Dun Boraige being thus a bi-lingual pleonasm.

SEMI-BROCHS.—DUN MOR VAUL. MASON-WORK, NORTH EXTERIOR OF MAIN FORT

SEMI-BROCHS,—DUN MOR VAUL.

GROUND GALLERY BETWEEN THE WALLS OF MAIN FORT.

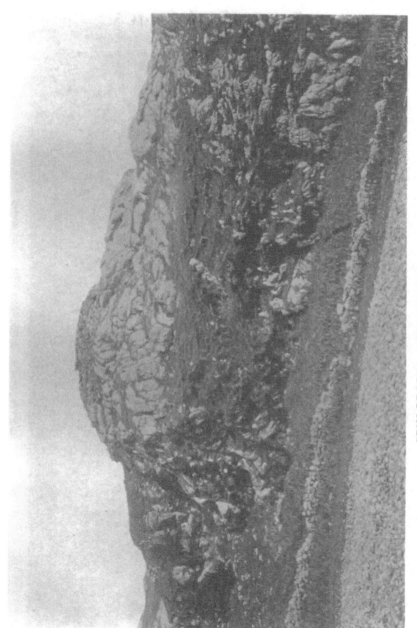

SEMI-BROCHS,—DUN HIADER, FROM WEST.

SEMI-BROCHS.—DUN HIADER FROM SOUTH.

the surface has been much disturbed within recent years,[1] the greater portion of its walls having fallen (or been thrown) down the steep rocks towards the sea at the north and the low ground to the south-west. The entrance to the main Dun has been on the north-east, and is still well-defined with large stones regularly built in at each side. It is 4 feet wide and 12 feet long, the latter measurement including both the outer and inner walls (each 51 to 54 inches thick), together with an intervening passage of from 30 to 36 inches in width, between these walls.

To the south-west, the inner wall again shows in the same dimensions, together with the exterior face of the outer wall, at a distance of 8 feet 3 inches, which, allowing 36 inches for the ground gallery, leaves 5 feet for the outer wall, and corresponds sufficiently with the more perfect portion on the opposite side.

The total diameter of the main Dun is about 65 feet externally, or 40 feet as to the interior, the lower courses of its outer wall being distinctly traceable almost continuously in more than half of its circumference. Within the central space natural rock outcrops, and traces are found of the foundations of stone huts (or cells), but no deductions could be formed as to these.

Upon the lower ground towards the south, and above the shore on the north-west, are portions of an outer protecting wall, while, near the entrance, appanages of the Dun seem to have extended northwards far over the rocks above the shore, thus including quite a large space.

[1] We were informed that Dun Boraige Mor and Dun Boraige Beg were both partially excavated by the present Duke of Argyll, at the same time as Dun Mor Vaul, about twenty years ago.

To the east, outside the entrance to the main fort are continuous traces of an exterior causewayed access two or three feet wide, leading up the slope and curving in from the south. This approach has been flanked upon both sides by walls, and on the north—between the access and the rocks—by a number of separate huts, some of them rectangular, but others probably circular, the whole enceinte being very well marked. Only a little pottery was to be seen (some with patterns) together with hammer-stones and a single piece of flint, also kitchen-midden bones (including a deer's horn), and shells, with a few horses' teeth.

Dun Boraige Mor is not within sight of Dun Hanais, the next large fort to the south-west, but, as is afterwards noted, a smaller intermediate Dun upon Cnoc Charrastaoin is visible from both of these.

Eastwards, quite near Dun Boraige Mor is Dun Boraige Beg, and again beyond it, to the north of Traigh Bail' a' Mhuilinn, stands Dun Beannaig, both clearly within view, and afterwards to be described.

The only other fort in Tiree still recognisable as distinctly of this class is DUN HIADER,[1] near the south-east corner of the island and midway between Hynish and Balaphuil—about a mile from each township. It occupies an exceedingly strong position upon the summit of a high rocky point close to the shore, and the

─────────

[1] *Hiader* is said to be the genitive of *Siadeir*, and merely a Gaelic corruption of the old Norse *setr* or modern *sœter*, signifying 'mountain pastures,' and hence 'a shieling.' 'Setter' in Orkney, and 'shader' in Lewis are common suffixes in place-names.

rough shingle on both sides of its base was in recent years a favourite place for kelp-burning.

This Dun shows a well-built double outer defence upon its north and only accessible side, where the entrance still exists through a gateway a yard in width, up a paved slope, although quite possibly this pavement was originally in the form of steps.

The main building measures some 50 feet in diameter including its double walls, 10 to 10½ feet across, upon the south and west. To the east these walls have merged into the solid and still higher rock, and there show a thickness of only 8½ feet, narrowing still more between that point and the entrance on the north side. From careful examination it is evident that round at least half the circumference of this Dun—from the south-east to the north-west—there has been a passage or ground-gallery, about 30 inches wide and 5 or 6 feet in height, running between the two concentric walls of the main building (each some 4 feet thick), but ceasing (if not *rising*) where the rock crops out in massive form on the east. To the west and south the ground gallery shows most clearly, and in several parts can be measured. The walls of the main fort are highest towards the south, six or seven courses of the outer portion (some 5 feet in height) still standing in position, while the interior wall (upon higher ground) commences at about the upper level of the outer, and reaches an elevation of nearly as much again, making a total from the exterior base of about 10 feet, which may perhaps give some indication of the original height of the structure.

Dun Hiader does not seem to have suffered by use as a quarry, although, from the numerous freshly fallen stones—especially to the south—it has evidently been much demolished through deliberate vandalism in very recent times. Within the enclosure, near the doorway, is one cell, with perpendicular walls (so far as shown), about 7 feet 6 inches in diameter; and there are traces of at least three others of apparently similar size and character. A very little pottery was found, together with bones (kitchen-midden refuse) and small rounded pebbles, and a single flint was noticed. Leaving the main Dun, its doorway (nearly 4 feet wide) is just traceable through the walls. Then comes the outer defence and narrow passage, with a steep zig-zag descent to the west and a wider and more gradual one to the east. Westwards, upon the other side of the deep gully, there seems to be a cleared pass through the rocks, near to, and somewhat parallel with the shore, continuing for more than a hundred yards, apparently roughly causewayed in the damper places, and ending between high rocks with traces of a barrier or portal across the roadway. From Dun Hiader is plainly visible Dun na Cleite near Hynish to the east, but Dunan Nighean to the west at Balaphuil cannot be seen.

Mr. J. Sands refers to the existence of a local rhyme, according to which Fionn (the Ossianic hero) left his gold in this Dun Hiader.[1]

Although the Duns which have just been described are all that can be recognised, with any distinctness, as being of the semi-

[1] *Proc. Soc. Antiq. Scot.*, vol. xvi. p. 461.

KELP-BURNING AT DUN HIADER, FROM WEST.

DUN HEANISH, FROM SOUTH.

Broch type, four at least may be added as showing some traces of the same character, while other four, too much dilapidated to be classed with any certainty, may also have been of similar structure. Those to which we refer are, in Class B, Dun Heanish, Dun Boraige Beg, Dun Vaul Beg, and Dun Hanais (so much ruined as to be quite indeterminate, unless possibly by thorough excavation), and in Class C (Marsh- or former Loch-Duns), Dun Beg a' Chaolais, Fang an t-Sithein, Carnan Liath, and Dun Ibrig. Of those mentioned in Class C the first three are simply large circular (apparently more or less artificial) mounds, and otherwise shapeless. Dun Ibrig shows a series of concentric walls, and thus comes very close to Class A.

CLASS B

ROCK-FORTS—usually close to the shore.

Recommencing near the north end of Tiree, we now take the second type of Dun, which, with few exceptions,[1] is totally different from that just described. The distinction may be broadly stated to consist in—*first*, the decidedly irregular outline of the defences, whether one or more lines are traceable; and *second*, the absence of any round central keep with its yard-wide passage or gallery between concentric walls.

Close to the north-east shore, half a mile south-west from Dun Mor a' Chaolais, and upon a point which divides Poll a' Chrosain from Traigh Crionaig, is DUN SGIBINIS,[2] immediately to the north ● 5

---

[1] At least four other Duns have just been noted as possibly belonging to Class A.

[2] *Sgibinis* is not Gaelic, but Norse for 'ship-point.' *Cf.* Skipness in Kintyre.

of a tiny natural harbour named Port Sgibinis. The seaward end of this small promontory is cut off from the land by a wall of large stones, showing distinctly in its centre an entrance 4 feet in width, after which comes part of the wall of the fort proper, also of massive build. The seaward side, where another wall has certainly stood, is now bare rock, but upon this lies one very large stone much exceeding a ton in weight.

Like almost all the other Duns, this has evidently been used as a quarry, even up to a recent date. Still it is a clearly marked site, although never large. Some pottery was to be seen, including good line-patterns, and also a few hammer-stones. An eye-witness told how, between the entrance and inner wall of the Dun, a flat place had been found paved with large pebbles on sand, and that some rams'-horns and pottery lay there,—apparently upon the hearth of a dwelling. A narrow causeway running up the hillside to the east, in a northerly direction towards Crois a' Chaolais, has already been described under Dun Mor a' Chaolais.

• 6   Next to be noticed is DUN OTTIR,[1] upon the island of Soa (which is not an island at extreme low water), nearly a mile south of Dun Sgibinis. The fort is not marked upon the 6-inch Ordnance map, nor indeed is it very distinguishable upon its actual site, a rocky point near the south end of Soa. Here are many loose stones, though apart from its traditional name this Dun is very unsatisfactory, being much ruined and overgrown, and presenting no definite traces of human occupation. The site

---

[1] 'Ottir' was a proper name among the Norsemen. 'Thorfinn, son of Otter,' was a Norwegian chief in the Sudreys, ca. 1150 (Skene's Celtic Scotland, vol. iii. p. 35).

is within view of Dun Mor a' Chaolais, Dun Sgibinis, Dun Gott, Dun an t-Sithein, and Dun Heanish. The island of Soa—very rugged towards the south, but in its northern portion fairly level —is edged upon the west, north, and east by raised beaches of water-worn stones at a considerable elevation above both the neighbouring surface and the present high-water mark.

Upon a rocky knoll at the north end of a small ridge known as CNOC CREAGACH, a quarter of a mile west from the ruined   • 7 Chapels at Kirkapol and near the north-east of Loch Riaghain, there seems to have been an unimportant fort, measuring only about 5 yards in diameter over both walls. Within are slight mounds, but much of its surface appears to have gone to build a large turf-dyke that crosses its south end, in which (where the soil is broken) are to be found small bits of old pottery. Further, it is not surprising to find no stones *in situ*, since the natural rock outcropping in the vicinity has also been quarried in very recent times, while among the debris in one such place were observed large unglazed potsherds. This site is within view of Dun an t-Sithein, Dun Balaphetrish, Dun Gott, and Dun Mor a' Chaolais, as perhaps also of Dun Mor Vaul. Close to the loch, in another old turf wall, are kitchen-midden ashes and pottery, probably from this Dun. Pottery is said also to occur at an island-rock in Loch Riaghain.[1]

---

[1] In Blaeu's Atlas of 1662 a place-name 'Weill' occurs midway between the site of the present manse and this Loch Riaghain, which however is there marked Loch Kirkabol, with an island near its centre, 'Ylen na Hyring.' 'The Wyle' or 'Woyll' is occasionally mentioned in old charters, but its position could not now be locally identified. The copy of 'An ancient Parochial Map of Scotland' reproduced in *Origines Parochiales* places 'Wyle'

Upon a small rocky point at Port nan Caorach, on the south shore of Gott Bay, some 300 yards east from the Manse (and chiefly within the glebe, of which the boundary wall crosses
• 8 through it) is DUN GOTT. The surface is of unbroken turf and rock, but this Dun remains fairly well defined to the extent of some 6 yards by 8, without any loose stones upon it, these having evidently all gone into the dyke. Dun Gott is in a direct line between Dun Mor a' Chaolais and Dun an t-Sithein.

Next, upon the south-east summit of Ben Gott, fully half a mile north-west from Scarinish (the port and chief village of Tiree)
• 9 is DUN AN T-SITHEIN [1] (*i.e.* 'the hillock of the fairies,' certainly not the true name). This stands half a mile from the nearest shore, and has been a very strong fort as regards its natural advantages of position. The remains of its walls are clearly to be traced upon the sides of the hill, but the surface of the summit is almost unbroken. A very little rude pottery, together with one hammer-stone, were the only relics found. Distinctly beyond the Dun, from the south base of the hill, runs a strong wall of very large stones and with the appearance of a gateway through it. Within this outer boundary, towards the south-east, are scattered

at the opposite side of the island, close to where Balaphetrish ought to appear. If both maps are correct (perhaps quite a gratuitous supposition), it may have been that 'The Wyle' extended right across the island, like 'The Reef' between Hynish and Balaphetrish Bays, farther south.

[1] See 'Fang an t-Sithein,' *postea.* In Iona are two mounds known as Sithean Mor and Sithean Beg, the former being mentioned in Adamnan's *Life of St. Columba* under the name of *Colliculus Angelorum* (Reeves' *Adamnan*, p. 219, where the editor notes a *Mons Angelorum* or *Carn Ingli* in Pembrokeshire). Two other *sithean* in Tiree are described in connection with Dun Ceann a' Bhaigh.

the ruins of three or four separate erections composed of large stones.

The fort itself completely covers the southmost of the three hills which form Ben Gott,—an oval knoll with precipitous rocks to the north and north-west, a wide gully dividing the Dun from the next eminence to the north. Half-way up the steep hillside on the south and west are the foundations of a stone rampart, which continues northwards for some distance and then joins on to a natural barrier of rock. Above this are in succession the remains of two inner walls at intervals of about 4 and 3 yards respectively, both of these also abutting upon the rock at the north-west; and upon the flat top there has been still another rampart enclosing an oval space of about 12 by 18 yards. A wall also shows high up on the east. The entrance has been by the north-east shoulder, the only point where the ascent is at all gradual.

Upon low-lying but rocky ground to the east, at a distance of some 25 and 100 yards, appear to have been two separate ancient buildings, possibly contemporary with the Dun. Upon the third and most distant (northerly) summit of Ben Gott seem also traces of some circular erections, and another smaller one occurs upon a much lower isolated knoll about 100 yards to the north-east. Dun an t-Sithein is within sight of Dun Heanish, Dun Ibrig, Dun Gott, and Dun Mor a' Chaolais, while its northern annexe has a view of Dun Balaphetrish.

Next in order comes DUN HEANISH, a mile south of Scarinish, • 10 upon the point which divides Traigh an Duin from the extensive

Bay of Hynish to the south. This fort is well defined in outline, and upon both its north and south sides the first course of the outer wall (of very large stones) still remains in position. The inner fortifications and arrangements are however most indistinct, having been much quarried even up to the present date. The general plan seems to primarily consist of a main fort, roughly circular and about 50 feet in diameter inclusive of its two separate concentric walls, which (with a probably intervening passage [1]) appear to have measured about 11 feet over both.

Completely enclosing this main building has been an outer defence at a greatly varying interval—about 8 yards as a rule, but diminishing on the west to little more than 2 yards— doubtless owing to the configuration of the site. Farther out, but only from the south to the north-east, is still another rampart at a distance of about 10 feet, thus giving to the fort a total dimension of some 90 by 110 feet over the outworks.

The exterior entrance seems to have been towards the south, while that to the main Dun was perhaps on the north-east—if so, it was apparently only 25 inches wide.

A little pottery was to be seen, some with a raised zig-zag pattern close to the rim, but chiefly with indented lines ; any hammer-stones were decidedly poor, but bones were plentiful (usually split, for the extraction of the marrow) and with them some kitchen-midden shells. Within view from Dun Heanish are Dun Mor a' Chaolais, Dun an t-Sithein, and the Dun upon Am Barradhu, as also probably Dun Ottir.

[1] Thus Dun Heanish ought possibly to come into Class A.

In connection (or at least in juxtaposition) with Dun Heanish is to be noted a unique feature. Immediately to its south, separated only by a narrow creek about 25 yards wide (usually dry at higher than half tide) is Eilean nan Gobhar,[1] from which, exactly opposite the Dun and running across the creek directly towards it, extends a ruined double wall or breakwater 5 yards wide, with very large stones in a distinct row at each of its edges, of which the westward (or inshore) is better defined than the eastward (or seaward) although both are clearly marked, and the space between them strewn with smaller stones. The length of this erection is some 20 yards, and there has evidently been a gap of 4 or 5 yards on the north (or Dun) side. Again, to the south-west of Dun Heanish a similar pier-like structure extends nearly two-thirds across the same tidal creek, but in this case from the land towards Eilean nan Gobhar, instead of *vice versâ*, leaving an unwalled space of some 10 yards next the island. Neither of these erections can have been meant for a pier, since both of them abut upon decidedly steep and awkward rocks, and it seems probable that they are to be explained as breakwaters by means of which a very safe harbour for small boats would be formed within the creek, although whether of ancient or later construction had better be left an open question.

Upon the west end of the rocky point Am Barradhu—at ● 11 that part precipitous though not very high—near the south-east

---

[1] 'The island of the Goats,' chiefly composed of bare irregular rocks, although there are a few grassy patches which may have been occupied.

extremity of Tiree and south of Hynish[1] Bay, is the outer wall of a Dun which has apparently (as regards its main fort) measured about fourteen by eighteen yards. Close on the south, at a slightly lower level but communicating with the central Dun, has been a small annexe, while further to the east, outwards upon the point, are traces of other walls. In this latter direction, however, the rock has been so much quarried in connection with the lighthouse station erected at Hynish for the service of Skerryvore[2] that any foundations are most indistinct.

In the main Dun a very little pottery was seen; a few flints and rounded pebbles also occurring both there and in a break in the turf towards the east. Fine specimens of patterned pottery have been found in former years near this fort, especially in a small cave above the shore to the south-east.

From the Dun at Am Barradhu (immediately above the disused powder-magazine) at least five others are visible, viz. those of Cleite, Heanish, an t-Sithein, Balaphetrish, and Mor a' Chaolais.

Nearly a mile west from Am Barradhu, upon a very large and steep rock (Cleit Beg) close to the south shore of Tiree, • 12 is DUN NA CLEITE,[3] which has been a strong fort covering the whole of a lofty rugged hill between one and two acres

---

[1] Here may be noted the great similarity between the names Heanish, Hynish, and Hanais, localities in Tiree separated from each other by several miles. The suffix 'nish' or 'ness' is clearly Norse for 'point.'

[2] Hynish was a busy place from 1836 to 1844 during the erection of Skerryvore lighthouse, but since about the year 1890 it has been abandoned except as a signal-station.

[3] Meaning 'Fort of the rocks,' *Klettr* being Norse for a rock or cliff. A similar word, *cleit*, occurs in Gaelic for an isolated rock, but is not in common use, being probably

DUN NA CLEITE, FROM SOUTH-EAST.

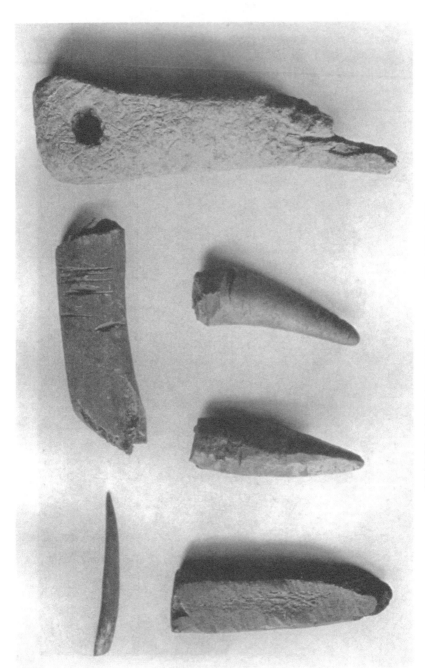

SHAPED BONES (ONE FROM COLL, SEE P. 43), ACTUAL SIZE.

in extent. It is by far the largest example of all the Duns in Coll or Tiree, the next in size being Dun Boraige Mor, and after that perhaps Dun nan Gall. The central portion is too rocky and irregular to have afforded much space for occupation, and yet in each small grassy nook are indications of one or more separate dwellings. The main buildings and chief entrance have been towards the north, at the end of a gully about 50 yards long which runs from south-east to north-west between the two hills Cleit Beg and Cleit Mor.[1] Both ends of this gap are walled across, as is also the east edge of the fort in two separate places on the face of Cleit Beg above the gully, although these form a small and not very important part of the Dun, seeing that its two accesses—the main one to the north-east and another to the south-east—are entirely outside and beyond the barriers which have crossed the rift between the two Cleits. These entrances are both distinctly traceable, but in each case so much ruined as scarcely to afford matter for description.

The fortifications of Dun na Cleite are visible at many

acquired from the Norse. *Cleit* indeed seems to be usually applied to skerries, of which four near the east shore of Tiree bear this name—Cleit Ruag, and Cleit Heanish, in Gott and Hynish Bays respectively, and two others marked simply 'A' Chleit' not far from Dun Heanish.

On the way to Dun na Cleite, a quarter of a mile west from the fort upon Am Barradhu and immediately to the west of Hynish farm-house, is a steep rocky hillock, Cnoc Mor, which may have been crowned by a Dun. If so, the entrance was certainly by its northern slope. Only a few loose stones could be found upon the summit, with absolutely no traces of walls. The finding of a good (but much weathered) hammer-stone close to its southern base is too meagre a clue to follow up.

[1] Cleit Mor was probably also occupied, but no very distinct traces could be recognised.

points, but the portion in best preservation is an inner wall on the west side, about half-way up the hill and immediately above the largest flat space which the fort has contained—a little south of the chief entrance.

Here, at a natural terrace between two turf-covered areas, are four courses of stones still in position, the upper row forming the lowest of another series of four tiers immediately to the south, these two overlapping fragments aggregating—at one point —a total of seven courses, equivalent to about 7 feet of height. In two or three places, especially on the east side, were kitchen-middens, containing bones (several bearing transverse cuts), shells, many small rounded pebbles, a flat and evidently shaped stone, pottery (including part of a very shallow dish, sufficient to show its form), with occasional patterned fragments (some with a raised zig-zag near the rim), as also broken hammer-stones, but not one of these latter really good. It seemed significant to discover in these kitchen-middens about a score of horses' teeth, a fact which suggests that the Dun-dwellers may have used horse flesh as an article of diet.[1] Three fragments of iron or metallic ore, a single nut, and four artificially shaped pieces of bone, nearly half an inch thick, squared or rounded, but in either case brought to a point—were also found, being unique in our experience of the Duns of Coll and Tiree.[2]

[1] See also Dunan Nighean in the same connection.

[2] Mr. Sands found here a piece of deer's horn with a cross rudely cut upon it (*Proc. Soc. Antiq. Scot.*, vol. xvi. p. 461). The same observer exhibited to the Scottish Society in 1883 a bronze sword and a very peculiar bronze swivel-headed pin, both of them found in Tiree, although the particular locality is not named (*Ibid.*, vol. xvii. p. 285).

About a hundred yards to the south-east of Cleit Beg, between the south side of Cleit Mor and the rocks above the beach, there has been a wall across a natural pass—perhaps a guarded approach as at Dun Hiader, though not quite so well marked. From Dun na Cleite are plainly visible Am Barradhu to the east, and Dun Hiader to the west.

A mile and a half north-west, close to the small village of Balaphuil,[1] upon a very irregular rocky point (or even, in the strictest sense, upon *two islands*) of somewhat awkward access over 'slocs' or small rifts through the rocks, is DUNAN NIGHEAN, or 'The little Fort of the Girls.'[2] The island (or peninsula) upon which this fort stood, is divided into two distinct sections, the intermediate rock or islet to the north-east, between the main Dun and the shore, having also on its summit the foundations of an old building, some 15 by 19 feet over the walls. The gaps which separate these islands from the shore and from each other are very narrow, the first measuring about 5 feet, and the second only half that width; but no doubt both of these would be bridged at the period when the Dun was occupied. In approaching the fort from the shore one has first to traverse the wider sloc and the smaller islet (with its subsidiary erection already noted),

[1] Literally 'the town of mud' evidently in connection with Loch a' Phuill, which is less than a mile to the north. Clay occurs in this neighbourhood, and it was at Balaphuil and at Sandaig (near the other side of the loch), that native 'craggans' were last made in Tiree.

[2] This name seems to be genuine. In the island of Mull, close to Loch na Keal, is another Dunan nan Nighean; while in North Uist is a fine symmetrical island fort (with a causeway) known by the still more circumstantial title of 'Dun nan Nighean righ Lochlinn,' or 'The Fort of the daughters of the King of Norway.'

and then, stepping across the narrower sloc, the main island is reached, up which the entrance follows a steep rocky rise of some 15 feet to the main Dun. Here, within an enclosure extending from side to side of the plateau, and measuring some 50 by 60 feet, the central Dun is shown as about 6 yards interior diameter, a few very large stones still remaining upon its surface.

Farther out, towards the south-west or seaward point of the island, are traces of one or two smaller erections upon lower ground.

A series of small kitchen-middens is disclosed for some length upon the north edge, containing fragments of pottery (a fair proportion patterned), many bones and shells, and some crab-claws, together with numerous small round pebbles (such as have been previously noticed) and some hammer-stones remarkable only for their rude shape. About a dozen teeth of the horse were found in this midden, a circumstance already observed at Dun na Cleite, and of not infrequent occurrence at similar sites in Tiree. Amongst the pottery were fragments of two very small cups, incomplete, though sufficient to show their shape and capacity—in both respects closely resembling the bowl of a modern wine-glass. In addition to the above were found one or two nuts, and two worked pieces of metal (apparently iron); also a number of bones of natural shape but with transverse cuts, and two artificially shaped bones, one with a hole through its thicker end, and the other sharpened at the point, as if for a boring tool. Only one flint was observed, and perhaps the best

'SLOC' OR GULLY AT DUNAN NIGHEAN.

KENAVARA POINT, FROM DUN HIADER.

find was a pottery-whorl[1] of $2\frac{1}{4}$ inches diameter, pierced by a quarter-inch hole and bearing evident marks of use. Two nodules of metallic ore were also disclosed, and clay exists in a most non-natural position upon the north side of the Dun, having evidently been collected for the manufacture of craggans, this being the only instance of the kind noticed throughout Tiree. We were informed that the upper stone of a quern was discovered upon this site.

Before leaving Dunan Nighean, some description must be attempted of a curious long and narrow passage which runs through the rocks at high-water mark for some 200 yards from south to north, commencing exactly at the north-east end of the Dun. Here, and for about half of its length, it has taken shape from a regular vertical 'fault' in the strata, averaging about 3 to 4 feet in width, although narrowing at one point to 19 inches. We were assured by a neighbouring cottar that this was formerly a roofed-in passage, with walls upon either side in those places where gaps occur in the natural stratification. This evidence seems perfectly credible, especially with the added fact that a second half of this gallery—through a sand-bank to the north, and running underneath a row of four cottages—still exists as a more or less hollow space, 4 or 5 feet in height. The passage is said to have emerged through a gap[2] (one of three) in the otherwise solid rock near the beach at the north-west end of

---

[1] Mr. John Sands unearthed three clay whorls from this Dun (*Proc. Soc. Antiq. Scot.*, vol. xvi. p. 461).

[2] Doubtless continuations or branches of the main fissure nearer the Dun.

the sand-bank. It was further added that in the sand close to
this northern exit, our informant's uncle found, a number of years
ago, a complete craggan of the capacity of about a gallon, bearing
several (perhaps three) distinct patterns upon its exterior.[1]

In a very remote spot—a mile and a half due west from
• 14 Dunan Nighean, but not in sight of it[2]—is DUN EILEAN NA BA,
off the extreme point of Kenavara, and in full view of its cliffs
looking north-west from the Dun. This fort, considering its
solitary and trackless situation, is disappointing as regards its
state of preservation. Indeed one is tempted to think that the
Tiree boys must have made a special point of spending their
Sunday afternoons in throwing down its walls—as is seriously
asserted in the case of Dun Hiader.

Dun Eilean na Ba (the Fort of the island of the cows), stood
upon the summit of a large irregular rock, which, before the
erection of a substantial causeway across a gully on its north, had
evidently been an island at high tides. This causeway or solid
bridge will measure, roughly speaking, about 5 feet in width,
3 feet high to the north, and 6 feet to the south where it joins
the island, with large stones in its base. Thence the entrance to
the fort, at the only accessible point from the land, is very steep.
The main Dun is upon the flat summit, but shows now the merest

---

[1] No such good fortune befell the writer as to find in any Dun even one fairly complete
craggan, patterned or unpatterned, although a small unpatterned pot was seen which was
dug out of Dun Acha in Coll, and has been mentioned in connection with that fort. Very
occasionally unpatterned craggans—of most varying size—could be acquired by gift or
purchase, but none of these seem to have come from the Duns, although one or two are from
the sandhills.

[2] This fort is, however, within view of Dun Hiader.

traces of foundations and a few fragments of outer wall above the precipitous gully to the north, into which very many of its stones have fallen. The chief plateau measures about 18 to 20 yards in diameter, and to the south is a smaller space which without doubt has also been occupied by buildings. Close to the south-west is a separate high rock, with marks of some erection upon it also. This rock is now only accessible by careful climbing, and is noticeable for a very luxuriant growth of wild celery.

Half a mile due north from Eilean na Ba,—but upon the west side of Kenavara Point,[1] and thus completely hidden from all the Duns on the south and east of Tiree, being visible apparently from none except Dun Hanais, three miles to the north,—is Dun nan Gall, 'the Fort of the strangers,' or 'foreigners.' ● 15 This name is unusual and significant in so far as regards the occupants of the fort, although easily explicable upon the very probable theory that the *Gall*[2] may have taken possession of it from the original builders.

This Dun occupies the summit and seaward slope of a large irregular peninsula lying approximately east and west, with sheer precipices towards both north and south, in which latter direction it faces the still higher cliffs of the Kenavara headland. Thus situated, the only artificial protection now observable (in addition to four or five courses of wall above the precipice to the north-east, near the sole point of access) are two or three courses of

---

[1] A re-duplication, *Ken* or *Ceann* being Gaelic for 'head.'
[2] The Norsemen were commonly so styled.

a stone rampart across the entrance upon the east or landward side, where the approach is over a narrow neck of junction, additionally guarded by a natural gully which has added distinctly to the strength of the Dun.

Within this first barrier is a second wall at a distance of about 2 yards, the doorway seeming to have been very near the north edge.   Coming now to the main enclosure, immediately within this second rampart are traces of one or more small buildings, probably guard-chambers.   Farther in are the foundations of three or four oval erections, though not all complete as to circumference.   One of these was so close to the northern precipice that its outer half has entirely vanished with the gradual erosion of the rock at the edge upon which it stood.

Near these small interior buildings, in a very damp black soil—the decayed remains of animal and vegetable matter—were found, with a few broken hammer-stones, some small round pebbles certainly taken thither by human agency, a little pottery (some patterned), together with bones, and one or two small lumps of metallic ore or slag.   But these kitchen-middens, owing to the general condition of decay, are among the poorest specimens of their class.   A noticeable find was a quartzite disc, about an inch and a half in diameter and three-eighths of an inch thick, flat on its two faces and worked all round the edge from one face only,—thus presenting the appearance of a large scraper, although the material is very different from that of the ordinary flint type.

The ravine to the north of Dun nan Gall bears the name

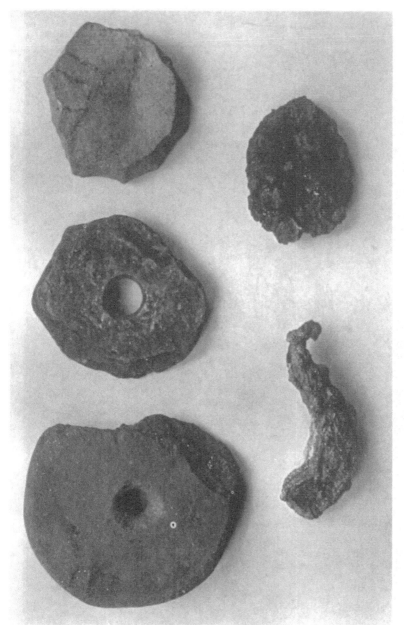

QUARTZITE DISC, AND WHORLS, ETC., ACTUAL SIZE. (SEE ALSO PP. 8, 95, 108, 134.)

DUN ON EILEAN DUBH.

'Sloc na h'Ursainn,'[1] and contains the remains of three or four separate erections, one at least of these being evidently circular and containing an inner oval of about 3 by 5 feet; the others may perhaps have been rectangular, but are not so clearly shown. Much debris from the Dun has fallen over the precipice into this gully, and among it were found one hammer-stone, a fragment of pottery, and a scrap of metal.

About 300 yards north from Dun nan Gall, upon an isolated and almost inaccessible rock called EILEAN DUBH, is a note- • 16 worthy fort marked on the Ordnance map as simply 'An Dun.'[2] This crowns the high islet separated from the shore to the south and east by narrow chasms—Sloc a' Cheim[3]—4 to 6 or more yards in width. Where bordered by the 'sloc' Eilean Dubh is quite precipitous. Upon two visits this Dun was found to be hopelessly inaccessible, but at the third—successfully timed for the extreme ebb of spring-tide—Eilean Dubh was no longer an island, the sea leaving even a small sandy beach to westward, while the slocs were passable at the expense of a slight wetting. The steep west side of the rock was climbed with little difficulty, though a much easier ascent was afterwards found from the north, where, near the base, is a natural (or aided) staircase in the rock. From this north side the Dun may have been accessible by wading, up to about half-tide. This, however,

[1] ? 'The Gully of the door-post.'

[2] 'The Fort.'

[3] The 'Gully of the leap,' evidently to be identified with the 'Leum Mhic a' Bhriuthainn,' across which one of the Browns of Tiree is said to have leapt backwards when pursued by a wild ox. (Rev. J. G. Campbell's *Clan Traditions and Popular Tales*, p. 17.)

must have been so intermittent an approach—especially in
stormy weather, and with a frequent surf—that it seems no idle
speculation to suggest that the ordinary entrance has been from
the south, over a drawbridge or plank across Sloc a' Cheim.
Indeed there seems to have been a doorway in the wall of the
Dun at the extreme south-east, which would fully substantiate
this theory.   Such an arrangement was evidently an absolute
necessity in the case of the completely precipitous Dun Cruit
(already described) off Lunga, one of the Treshnish Isles.

The extreme measurements of this Dun seem to have been
about 72 by 50 feet at the widest; on the south the wall has
been about 5 feet thick, and several courses still stand on the
north side.   The surface is very rankly overgrown, but shows
indications of walls within, probably the foundations of two or
three rude huts.   Some tiny pieces of pottery were found, one of
which is apparently patterned.

Eilean Dubh is not visible from Dun nan Gall although so
near to it, but is within sight of Dun Hanais, next to the north.

Nearly three miles to the north, upon Rudha Hanais, a
jutting point at the north end of Traigh Thodhrasdail, are the
• 17   scanty remains of DUN HANAIS.   As now seen, this Dun
consists of a large and evidently artificial mound, some 4 yards
above the surrounding level.   Towards the south are portions
of distinct walls on both sides, the diameter of the main erection
seeming to have been about 56 feet over its ramparts.   The
entrance appears to be upon the west, flanked outside by another
wall at a distance of 2 yards.   An exterior irregular rampart

seems to have existed, measuring 35 yards across the whole space enclosed. Dun Hanais is within sight of Dun nan Gall and of the fort next to be mentioned upon Cnoc Charrastaoin. Its type is now untraceable—unless perhaps by a thorough excavation—but it may not improbably have been a semi-Broch similar to Dun Mor Vaul.

Passing over another possible but most unsatisfactory site, a mile and a half due west from Dun Hanais and half a mile south of Hogh farmhouse—a large but irregular mound in a somewhat marshy place, as to which there is practically nothing more to be said—the next Dun is upon Cnoc Charrastaoin,[1] a • 18 rocky hillock at the shore about midway between Dun Hanais and Dun Boraige Mor, fully a mile north-east of the former and nearly half a mile south-west of the latter, being in view of both forts, which are not within sight of each other. The remains of this Dun are very indistinct, but upon the west of its summit could be traced 12 yards of a semi-circular wall composed of quite small stones. Several flints and two fragments of pottery were found upon its surface. This site is in view of Dun nan Gall in addition to the two others above-mentioned.

Upon some rocks 300 yards to the west (marked *Carrastaoin* on the Ordnance map) were to be seen flints in abundance, some pottery and hammer-stones, as also two kitchen-middens with shells and bones. These appear to have been unfortified dwellings, and there are indications of an ancient burial near.

---

[1] *Staoin* is Gaelic for 'juniper,' and *caora-staoin* for 'juniper berries.' The place-name Carrastaoin may however be more probably derived from *carragh* 'a rock,' and *staon* 'bent or awry,' thus meaning 'the crooked rock,' or possibly even 'the juniper rock.'

Half a mile north-east from Cnoc Charrastaoin (and only 300 yards east of Dun Boraige Mor, already described) is DUN BORAIGE BEG, which both in situation and condition bears much the same relation to its more massive and characteristic neighbour and namesake as does Dun Beg Vaul to Dun Mor Vaul.

● 19

The Dun stands upon quite a low rocky point, close to and not much above the level of the sea, which surrounds it upon all sides except at an isthmus on the south. Indeed at spring-tides it must have been temporarily an island, but for an artificial causeway, of which there seemed to be traces. Immediately above the shore, close to the only access, is a small well, evidently that of the Dun.

This fort is quite near the township of Bail' a' Mhuilinn (pronounced 'Balavulin' and meaning 'the town of the Mill') immediately to the south of the wide sandy beach which bears the same place-name—Traigh Bail' a' Mhuilinn. It has evidently suffered much from this proximity, owing to its convenience for use as a quarry, and upon each visit was found strewn with tangle laid there to dry, a number of kelp-kilns also existing between the main fort and its outer entrance. These circumstances will sufficiently account for the very ruinous condition of the Dun,—indeed, a crofter assured us that within his recollection the wall at the entrance was as much as 20 feet high, where now stand only four or five courses with a total height of about 5 feet, and that in a very small portion. Twenty feet must evidently be an exaggeration, especially as this wall (although with some huge stones in its base) does not appear to have been very thick. To the east, double walls are distinctly traceable, their faces about 9 feet apart; but both walls seem to have been narrow, and they converge towards the south—gradually approaching each other until they appear to unite into a single wall at each side of the entrance. The whole Dun measures about 18 yards in diameter including walls. Of its ancient occupation no relics were to be found except a very little pottery, a few bones and one or two hammer-stones.

In full view of Dun Boraige Mor and Dun Boraige Beg, half a mile north-east from the latter, upon a rock immediately above the farther end of the sandy bay, are the scanty remains of DUN BEANNAIG.[1] This fort has occupied the fairly level central summit, ● 20 measuring some 9 yards over its walls, which can still be traced. There appear to have also been some subsidiary buildings upon the lower sand-blown portion at the north-west, towards which a short but steep pathway has descended from the Dun proper. Above a small gully on the south side of the rock are kitchen-midden remains, occurring sparsely among sandy soil. Here were found shells, bones, round pebbles, and a very little patterned pottery.

To the north-east again, upon the crest of another division of the same hillock, is a more distinct kitchen-midden, lying upon the bare rock some 18 inches below the present surface of the turf. Here is disclosed in section a thin layer of bones and shells with a few fragments of pottery and of hammer-stones,

[1] Possibly 'the Dun at the corner.'

but so slender a stratum—in parts only one or two inches thick—
as to suggest that this portion of the site can only have been
occupied for a brief period.

The adjoining extensive and elevated sandbank of Balamhuilinn (afterwards to be specially noticed among the Sandhill
sites) completely intercepts all view from Dun Beannaig towards
the east, in which direction, at the distance of almost four
• 21   miles,[1] is the next fort to be mentioned—DUN BALAPHETRISH.[2]
This is—or more strictly speaking, was—upon the steep west
summit of the hill of the same name, a little to the south-east
of the modern farmhouse.   The Dun has certainly been both
large and strong, apparently measuring, with the outworks,
some 43 by 35 yards, if it included the whole flat top of the

---

[1] This is a much wider separation than is usual between the Tiree Duns, and probably
other forts exist (or have existed) between Dun Beannaig and Dun Balaphetrish, although
none could be discovered.

[2] 'The fort of the town of Patrick.'   In Martin's *Description of the Western Islands of
Scotland*, second edition, 1716, p. 270, is said of Tiree or *Tiriy*,—'There are several Forts
in the Isle ; one in the middle of it, and *Dun-Taelk* in *Baelly Petris*,'—and, consistently with
this description, one of the two place-names marked upon the accompanying 'new map'
(the other being *Soroby*) is *B. Petris*, although shown near the south end of the island where
Balaphuil really stands.   Probably this is due to some confusion between the two *Bal*-s,
Balaphetrish and Balaphuil, and Dun Taelk or something similar may have been the old
name of one of the two Duns at Balaphetrish.   It may not be too far-fetched to note that
Takt was the name of a son of King Brian Boroimhe (or *Boru*) of Ireland, who was with his
father at the battle of Clontarf in 1014 when King Brian was slain (*Burnt Njal*, vol. ii.
pp. 323, 337).   *Munch*, p. 59, states that Tadc, Tadg, or Teige, was a not uncommon
Irish name, especially in the O'Brian family.   Furthermore, the Gaelic form of Hugh is
Aedh, and in that language a *t* (euphonic) 'is placed between the article and substantive
nouns singular of the masculine gender, and in the nominative or objective case beginning
with a vowel' (Macleod and Dewar's *Gaelic Dictionary*, 1893 edition, p. 557).   In O'Reilly's
Irish Dictionary, Tadg is given as 'Thady, a man's name.'

hill. Of its structure there are now practically no remains except a few very large stones upon the west edge. At the same point can be seen traces of a narrow zig-zag pathway up the side of the steep rock from the north-west, although the main entrance was by an approach on the more gradual slope to the north-east, where some small bits of pottery and one fragment of flint were noticed.

Near the south of what may be judged to have been the area of the main fort still exists a very peculiar feature—a built well, upon the highest part of the hill. Steps lead down into this well, which is constructed of good masonry, so regular that if the stones are unhewn (which seems to be the case), they have been most carefully selected to fill their relative positions.

Dun Balaphetrish is a quarter of a mile from the shore, and exactly half a mile to the north, upon a small point at Port Ban, is another 'AN DUN' of the Ordnance Survey map. This small ● 22 fort has no specific local name, so far as could be gathered. It is conspicuously green, and although much ruined is still tolerably well-defined, containing within its centre a circular foundation of about 9 yards interior diameter. There is some appearance of another round enclosure outside, a little south of the fort itself. The surface of both is of unbroken turf with stones interspersed; one or two broken hammer-stones were seen at the Dun, but not a scrap of pottery was visible, although a small piece was noticed in a field quite near.

Two miles north-east from Balaphetrish, upon the rocky west point of Vaul Bay, and not a quarter of a mile due east from Dun Mor Vaul (already described as a semi-Broch) is DUN BEG VAUL. ● 23

This consists of a large and high circular mound—a flattened cone—which, at least in part, is probably artificial. The summit must have an elevation of 30 feet above the level and measure fully thrice as much in superficial diameter, containing towards the south-east an inner circle (no doubt the main fort) of 38 feet, with walls 5 feet thick. Nowhere are more than the merest foundations to be traced, except three courses of wall upon the top of the rock at the south-east edge, and one or two courses of two separate walls on the south-west side, the outer of these at the base of the mound and the inner about half way up its side. Although so much ruined this Dun has evidently been of elaborate construction, the whole surface of its steep sides being strewn with stones (none of them very large) which project through the turf. A strong natural protection is given by the precipitous rocks to the north and east, the latter showing also slight remains of walls. Upon the northern portion of the summit are traces of several small separate buildings, one of them 2½ yards in diameter.

Only a very little pottery (a single piece patterned) with some kitchen-midden shells and bones and a few rude hammer-stones were to be found. Dun Beg Vaul is within view of Dun Mor Vaul, An Dun at Salum, and Dun Mor a' Chaolais.

Immediately to the south of this Dun, between it and a cottar's house, is the distinct site of a very small circular building, 6 feet over the walls but of only 42 inches interior diameter. A little farther to the south-east, running eastwards between natural rocks, seems to be a made roadway, somewhat similar

DUN BEG VAUL, FROM SOUTH-WEST.

CLACH A' COILE, OR 'KETTLE STONE.'

to those which have been noticed in like association at Dun
Borbaidh in Coll, and Dun Hiader and Dun na Cleite in Tiree.
Upon the eastward shore, between rocks just above Vaul Bay,
may have been another much narrower approach, which certainly
now forms a convenient access through the otherwise very rough
and irregular surroundings.

In sight of Dun Beg Vaul, fully a mile to the east at the far
end of Salum Bay, is an isolated rock (an island at high-water)
known as AN DUNAN, or 'the little Fort.' This has literally • 24
been a very small Dun, without much strength save for the
intermittent protection given by its semi-insular position.
There is, however, one most interesting feature in the shape
of a massive shoreward causeway, about 5 yards wide and 60
yards in length. Of the fort itself nothing can be traced
except a few fragments of wall above the end of this causeway.
Thanks to the past efforts of a colony of rats, there were
disclosed some kitchen-midden bones, fragments of pottery, and
a very few hammer-stones, these latter including a rude specimen
in quartz (an unusual material) and another stone of peculiar
type—oval in shape and ten inches long, with an artificial round
depression worn in the centre of each of its flattish sides.

Half a mile to the north-east is Fhadamull, a level peninsula
—indeed nearly an island—with some appearance of a causeway
from the shore on the south.

From the 'Dunan' at Salum is a somewhat wide transition
to DUN CEANN A' BHAIGH, the last fort to be enumerated of • 25
the present class. This Dun, situated in Kenovay (the name

of this township being simply the same words in a corrupted form, meaning 'the head of the bay') is in the centre of Tiree, nearly equidistant between Balaphetrish Bay on the north and Traigh Bhagh on the south, about a mile from either shore, and is thus the most inland of all the Tiree Duns. This is but a poor specimen, with slight remains of a wall upon its summit towards the south-west of the long irregular ridge upon which it stood. Tradition states that this was the chief Dun of the island, where the general armoury was placed, and that it was demolished about thirty years ago for the sake (as usual) of building material for dykes. This story (as to its latter portion) received a curious quasi-confirmation from the fact that a good hammer-stone was found in a wall at the nearest croft to the north. The hillock has outcropping rock, and appears to be entirely natural. A few small fragments of pottery were noticed both upon the Dun and in a neighbouring field, as also some kitchen-midden shells, and a bit of shaped iron. Within view are Dun nan Gall, Dun Balaphetrish, Dun an t-Sithein, and the Dun on Am Barradhu.

Two hundred yards to the north-west are two grassy mounds, certainly artificial and probably sepulchral—named 'Da Sithean,' or 'the two fairy-knolls.' Of these the larger is about 5 feet high and 24 feet in diameter, the smaller measuring about 3 feet in height by 15 in diameter. Neither of these is complete, soil having been removed from both.

Before leaving Class B, it may be mentioned that very possibly there was a Dun of this character at Poll Odhrasgair, half way across the east end of 'The Reef,' between Baugh and Balaphetrish, upon a rocky ridge close to the north of a large pool formed by the burn 'An Fhaodhail.' Here has been a round erection about 10 feet in diameter, with walls only 2 feet thick. This, however, is too small to be accepted as a definite site.

The place-name 'Cnoc Eibrig' (not to be confounded with Cnoc Ibrig, or Dun Ibrig), at the shore immediately to the west of Baugh, may indicate a former Dun or *Borg*, but no traces could be found to justify more special notice.

An islet, 'Librig Mor,' off the north-east coast of Tiree, near Port Ban, Caoles, may prove to be another site, although a full examination was found to be impracticable.

Class C

Loch or Marsh Duns, upon Large Mounds

In Tiree there have been four forts of this type, all unfortunately (like the single specimen in Coll of the same class) now of quite indeterminate structure, with the exception of Dun Ibrig, which is in much better preservation than any of the others. All four, indeed, ought perhaps to have been included among the semi-Brochs of Class A.

Dun Beg a' Chaolais is about a mile north-west from Dun ● 26 Mor a' Chaolais, and distant about a quarter and half a mile respectively from bays upon the north-west and north-east of Tiree. This large mound (about 35 yards in diameter on the summit, with slopes of 8 yards in addition, and of

a present height of at least 15 to 20 feet) has been much
worked as a quarry for building purposes, no regular walls
being now distinguishable, while the stones and debris (as can be
seen wherever the surface is broken) have evidently been turned
over and shifted from their original position. The access has
been from the east, through the margin of a former loch
which has surrounded the Dun, and is still traceable as an
elevation, perhaps originally a causeway. Kitchen-midden bones
and shells are to be found, although not plentiful so far as
could be ascertained.[1] A fair amount of pottery occurs, with
some good patterns, but the chief feature of this fort was the
profusion of hammer-stones, including many large and one
of special form—that of a rude wedge, with evident marks of
use. There is no natural rock at any part, the whole mound
being apparently artificial.

Towards its east edge grows in abundance a noticeable plant—
Inula Helenium, or *Elecampane*, according to some authorities
indigenous to Britain, and formerly held in high medical repute.
Locally, its root is credited with beneficial effects upon the lungs
of horses,[2] and it seems quite possible that the plant may have
been cultivated for its medicinal qualities.

[1] In 1897 Lord Archibald Campbell here unearthed a polished piece of deer-horn
about three inches in length and somewhat decayed, but with a distinct barb, and presumably
a fish-spear or harpoon.

[2] The same plant occurs upon walls—usually of stackyards and always close to some
present or former croft,—in several localities in Tiree, though chiefly towards the south end
of the island. There can be little doubt that it was purposely cultivated in these places,
and is not a mere garden escape. It was observed (always in small quantity and invariably
in these positions) near Gott Bay, at Cornaig Beg, near Kilkenneth, in Mannel, and upon
two or three separate sites both in Balamartin and Balaphuil.

Towards the shore, at the north, is a large and wide raised beach which has served as a natural embankment to the former loch. This mound has in recent times been pierced by a deep cutting, through which the water is now completely drained off.

Next to be noticed is a very similar site, locally known as FANG AN T-SITHEIN,[1] three-quarters of a mile south-west from Dun Beg a' Chaolais and nearly half a mile south-east of Salum.

● 27

Its summit is about 12 feet above the level, and the whole mound measures some 43 yards across, inclusive of both slopes. Natural rock shows through its surface in massive form, and this indeed is its chief distinction from Dun Beg a' Chaolais. There is also a somewhat better marked terracing upon its sides, and the surrounding moat[2] is exceedingly well-defined, 8 or 9 yards in width and enclosed by a low modern dyke. No large stones remain *in situ*, and but few smaller ones are to be seen, the grassy surface being entirely unbroken. It was only at the extreme edge adjoining the cultivated moat, and in a neighbouring turf-dyke, that some small fragments of pottery and a single flint were found; several hammer-stones also lay within the enclosure.

[1] A Gaelic name, signifying 'the enclosure (or *fank*) of the Fairies,' merely an instance of the very common folk-lore association of 'the Fairies' with distinct green knolls, when the original purpose of these is unknown to the country people. See also Dun an t-Sithein (on Ben Gott, *antea*) and 'Da Sithean' in Kenovay. Fang an t-Sithein is not locally considered as a fort, but such it evidently has been, bearing in general character a strong resemblance to Dun Beg a' Chaolais.

[2] It is perhaps hardly correct to describe this as a 'moat,' much of its character being given by the surrounding wall, erected to protect the crofter's best patch of soil—containing, as it does, much refuse from the Dun. In ploughing this plot, flints and fragments of pottery are turned up.

There may have been an entrance from the east, where the moat is slightly raised, but in any case we were assured that there was formerly a causeway on the west, (towards the Salum crofts) although this is now untraceable. Adjacent in the latter direction is a large low-lying area, evidently formerly under water, as was certainly the case at Dun Beg a' Chaolais. Both of these forts are in secluded positions without much general view.

● 28   DUN IBRIG [1] (of the Ordnance map, or, as locally known, *Dun a' Bhaigh*) is a mile south-west of Scarinish and about half that distance north from the nearest shore at Baugh. Dun Ibrig stands upon a slight mound surrounded by a marsh which is said even now to become a loch in winter. It has been a large fort with an approach from dry and comparatively high ground to the south, but the remains consist of little more than four distinct concentric walls (built of large stones) occupying a total area of fully 40 yards in diameter, assuming the outer enclosure to be symmetrical although it follows the outline of an island within the marsh or shallow loch. The main fort measures about 18 feet across its interior, and 38 feet in

---

[1] Perhaps *Ibrig* may be 'Island Fort,' from the Norse. After much consideration, however, the present writer inclines to the belief that the 'Isleborg' of ancient Scottish charters is more probably to be identified with the island-fort formerly existing in Loch an Eilean and mentioned at the close of this chapter. If this latter identification be well-founded, it remains to be suggested that Ibrig and Eibrig (pronounced respectively *Eebrich* and *Aybrich*) may be bi-lingual compounds meaning 'the west fort' (*iar-borg*) and 'the east fort' (*ear-borg*). Cnoc Eibrig has already been noted at the end of Class B as the possible site of a fort, and reference is again made to it in Chapter XII. dealing with Sandhill sites in Tiree.

exterior diameter, this difference of 20 feet being accounted for by walls measuring from 8 to 12 feet across at each side. These are apparently double walls, the inner about 3 to 3½ feet thick, while allowance for an intervening 30 to 36 inch passage or ground-gallery would give to Dun Ibrig the leading characteristic of Class A. These walls of the central fort are however so much ruined and turf-grown that their dimensions could not be ascertained with any approach to precision, for which a thorough excavation would be necessary. The doorway of the main building is towards the east, and beyond, at an interval varying from 2 yards on the north to 5 yards on the south-west, is a *third* wall, with again a *fourth* some 3 yards farther out. Encircling this *fourth* wall (counting the double wall as two) is still another outer rampart beyond a clear space of 8 or 9 yards, these measurements applying specially to the southern portion of the whole fort. The exterior entrance, from the south, runs in a direct line through all the three outer walls, then turning eastwards to the doorway of the inner Dun.

Within the middle interval—that is, the narrow space of about 3 yards between the third and fourth walls, as above noted—are traces of several small circular stone huts of from 5 to 8 feet interior diameter, one situated immediately opposite the outer entrance and evidently having served as a guard-room.

The inner fort now contains three very small enclosures, each about 2 feet square (inside), one of the three being particularly distinct. These however may be marks of a secondary use of the Dun.

Only a single hammer-stone was found (occurring in a neighbouring turf-dyke to the east), while very few kitchen-midden bones or bits of pottery (one fragment patterned) were seen; but this is scarcely surprising as the whole surface (apart from the walls, which are also grass-grown) consists of un-broken turf.

Dun Ibrig is clearly within view of Dun an t-Sithein, Dun Balaphetrish, and Dun Ceann a' Bhaigh, as also probably of others.

Towards the south of Tiree, between Heylipol and Barrapol, half a mile east from Moss Church, is a large green mound some 20 yards in diameter, its summit apparently not more than about 9 feet above the level of the surrounding marsh. This • 29 is known as CARNAN LIATH, or 'the little grey cairn,' a name which has ceased to be descriptive, as no stones now remain upon its surface. The access has probably been from slightly higher ground to the east. In a turf-dyke adjoining to the east were seen a few kitchen-midden shells, with a large but rude hammer-stone lying near. This site is in view of Dun Ceann a' Bhaigh, Dun Balaphetrish, and Dun an t-Sithein.

Reference has already been made (after Dun Hanais, No. 17, Class B) to a very problematical Dun, although possibly of this type, upon Hogh Farm.

Class D

Duns upon Islets in Fresh-Water Lochs

Of this class only three (or possibly four) are to be enumerated in Tiree.

Towards the west end of Loch na Gile, about a mile north-east from Dun Balaphetrish and within view of that fort, has been an Island Dun in shallow water about 20 yards out from the south shore, with the merest traces of a former causeway. This islet is partly natural, containing a flat rock; and upon the grassy surface are distinct traces of buildings, with many separate stones also under water around its margin.

Upon the north-east edge are the remains of a strong outer wall enclosing a slighter inner erection some 7 yards in length, the distance between these two walls being about 6 feet. This Dun, however, can scarcely have been of any great strength or importance; a remark which applies to most of the present class.

Nearly half a mile to the north, upon the sea-shore at Port Cam Beg is a large poised rock locally known as Clach a' Coile, or 'the kettle stone,' a name derived from the fact that when struck by a small stone it gives forth a peculiar metallic or tinkling sound. Upon the top of this rock are many small cavities resembling cup-markings, though their origin may obviously be attributed to the continuous series of experiments made upon its 'ringing' qualities.

● 30

Both to the north and south of Port Cam Beg are raised beaches very similar to one noticed at Dun Beg a' Chaolais, and to others between that fort and the island of Fhadamull.

The next island-site is near the centre of the north side of **• 31** LOCH NA BUAILE, a small loch (now much reduced in extent by drainage) half a mile due south from Ben Gott with its Dun an t-Sithein. Here still exist the remains of a causeway, about 12 yards in length, connecting this island with a small point towards the east, and upon this promontory, opposite the causeway and at a distance of other 12 yards, are the foundations of a circular erection measuring 8 to 10 yards over its walls—no doubt, as is not unusual elsewhere, a subsidiary building in connection with the island-fort, of which the dimensions appear to have been about 7 by 8 yards.

In Loch Bhasapol (a sheet of water about half a mile wide in each direction) in Kilmoluag, just to the south of the Cornaig sandhills, are two islets, marked upon the Ordnance map **• 32** EILEAN MHIC CONUILL and Eilean Aird na Brathan. The first-named is formed of loose stones, being evidently artificial, and certainly the site of an old Dun, with many large stones in the water around it. There are said to be the remains of a causeway towards the north-west, but of this—without the aid of a boat—no traces could be found near the shore. Two flints were discovered in the low bank on the nearest point to the north, together with a few hammer-stones; while, a little to the east, on the margin of the loch, lay a stone-sinker, much weathered but with a distinct groove round its middle.

The second island, close to the east shore, may very likely be at least partly artificial, and have also had its Dun. Both are now occupied by shelters for wild-fowl shooting.

In Loch an Eilean at Heylipol[1] was formerly a castle upon an islet, but whether a Dun of Class D or a fortress of mediæval times can scarcely now be decided.[2] This castle at one period had its access from the shore by a drawbridge, and at another by stepping-stones or perhaps a causeway, but the whole building was demolished in 1748 for the erection of a mansion which is now the factor's residence and known as Island House. Perhaps at the same time, but not later than the year 1794, the intervening space was filled up with stones and soil,[3] and now the site is no longer an island but a peninsula. Built into the south wall is a stone inscribed 'A^DA 1748' (Archibald,

---

[1] To quote Beeverell's *Les Delices de la Grand' Bretagne*, Leyden, 1727, vol. vi. p. 1452, as to Tiree or 'Tyrryf,' 'Elle a un port assez bon, deux Lacs d'eau douce avec une Ile à châcun, qui est habitée. Celle du Lac Méridional, nommé *Hyrbol*, est occupée par un petit Château.' Hyrbol is certainly Heylipol, but which was the other loch with its inhabited island is hard to understand. Loch Bhasapol would almost seem indicated, being the only large loch in Tiree north of Heylipol, but the 'inhabited island' of 1727 is rather tantalising, if correct.

Blaeu's *Atlas* (of 1662) shows a castle upon an island, 'Ylen na Hyring,' in Loch Riaghain, there named 'Loch Kirkabol,' and considerably magnified. Upon the same map another 'Hyring' is marked in Hynish, near the site of Dun na Cleite. This last-named *Hyring* is doubtless to be identified with the *Herne* or *Herene* of *Reg. Mag. Sig.* 1496 and 1540, and also of the *Retours* in 1603 (Argyll, No. 7). *Herne* is shown upon a map in *Origines Parochiales*, vol. ii. part I.

[2] According to the *Statistical Account* of 1794 this castle was 'similar' to that of Breacacha in Coll, and therefore mediæval; but implicit reliance can hardly be placed upon this incidental description. The same authority states that Tiree had then '24 lakes, covering about 600 acres, some of which might be easily drained.'

[3] See the original *Statistical Account*, vol. x. p. 402.

third Duke of Argyll), evidently from the structure of that date, although the house has since been altered and enlarged.

'Isleborg,' already noted in connection with the name of Dun Ibrig (No. 28) near Baugh, appears to refer either to that fort or to the ancient castle which existed in Loch an Eilean. 'Island Castle' would indeed be a literal rendering of 'Isleborg.' Gregory, in his *History of the Western Highlands*, p. 126, mentions the death, *ca.* 1519, of Sir Donald (*Galda*) of Lochalsh as having occurred at either Cairnburg or 'the Inch of Teinlipeil in Tyree.'[1]

In the whole of Tiree there are but few islands—even including the marsh-forts, Dun Ibrig, etc.—from which to choose, and the balance of evidence for identification with 'the Inch of Teinlipeil' seems certainly—and with 'Isleborg' very probably —to lie in favour of the ancient fort or castle in Loch an Eilean. The name Teinlipeil is now quite unknown in Tiree, although that of 'Templefield' occurs near Loch an Eilean. Perhaps it is not too far-fetched to suggest that 'the Inch of Teinlipeil' may have possibly been a corruption of 'Innis tighe ann a' Heylipol.'

Isleborg (as already has been mentioned in Chapter VIII. upon the Treshnish Isles) was coupled with Cairnburg in a charter of 1390, while a century later both of these castles, together with other three in the Sudreys, were up to the year 1493 in the hereditary keeping of Hector Odhar, ninth chief of Clan Maclean, who possessed a great part of Mull and Tiree.[2]

---

[1] See also *Collectanea de Rebus Albanicis*, p. 324.   [2] Gregory, p. 69.

ISLAND HOUSE.

SCARINISH HARBOUR, FROM WEST.

In our national records, *Iseleborgh* seems to be first mentioned in a charter granted by David II. at Ayr, 12 June 1343,[1] which includes also Kernoborgh and Dunchonall.

[1] Robertson's *Index of Charters,* p. 100. No indication of a specific locality is anywhere given to Isleborg in the ancient documents, but according to *Origines Pàrochiàles,* vol. ii. p. 322, this castle appears in 1354 under the name of *Hystylburch* ; a suggestion being added in a footnote that 'it may possibly have been the old castle whose ruins remain on the isle of Scerna,' one of the Treshnish group, (?) the modern *Sgeir a' Chàisteil.* There is certainly every probability that Isleborg was in either the Treshnish Isles or Tiree.

CHAPTER XI

TIREE—SITES OF ANCIENT INLAND DWELLINGS

THE special class of circular stone-huts, upon somewhat artificial knolls, tentatively suggested in Chapter III. on Coll, seems to be entirely absent in Tiree, at least at the present day.

A few sites may here be mentioned which appear to have been occupied by more than simple shielings. These are situated for the most part in scattered groups near Loch Cnoc Ibrig and Loch na Buaile, within little more than half a mile south from Dun an t-Sithein,[1] and the best examples occur upon the summits of rocky mounds of no great elevation, with also a notable absence of any traces of fortifications.

Perhaps the best group is upon Cnoc Ibrig, a small ridge immediately to the south-west of the loch which bears the same name, and about half a mile north from Dun Ibrig which has already been described. Here is a row of three circular enclosures, each showing as a slight mound, and a little to the east, upon the same 'Cnoc' are to be seen traces of two others (one of somewhat rectangular shape), with a raised pathway from one to another and continuing northward to the loch-side which is

[1] Several have already been noticed in the close neighbourhood of this Dun, and to these no further reference is here made.

very near. Between the two last mentioned sites was found a large flint-chip lying upon the bare rock. It must however be admitted that these eastward sites may simply be the ruins of an abandoned croft.

To the south-east of Loch na Buaile are the remains of two similar erections, distant from the loch about 50 and 300 yards respectively. The latter is close to the east of a tiny loch, and part of the wall is quite traceable, with large stones in the foundations, the building appearing to have been sub-circular, and measuring about 20 by 25 feet.

In the neighbourhood of Loch na Buaile are at least three other round erections, varying from seven to ten feet interior diameter, but these have evidently been latterly used as small sheep-folds if not really built for that purpose.

Another series of sites—notable for an abundance of flint— has already been mentioned as existing at Carrastaoin, a little to the east of the Dun upon Cnoc Charrastaoin.

Upon the high ground about half way between Dun Hiader and Hynish, near the south-east point of Tiree, is a rectangular enclosure as of a building, but this is perhaps only worth mention- ing on account of the existence near it of a number of huge upright blocks of stone, standing almost in a regular row.

On the south-east of Kenavara, near the path to Temple- Patrick, is another old site upon meadow ground above the shore. In the centre of this lies one very large stone.

Half a mile south-east from Hogh farmhouse is a nondescript but remarkable building in fair preservation, which may however be of modern origin, and susceptible of some ready explanation. This stands east and west upon a knoll, its east side being a massive straight-edged rock, which also forms one of the walls of the entrance, a narrow passage only 16 inches in width and fully 3 feet long. The other walls are built of comparatively small stones, the interior measurements being about 7 feet in length by 4 feet 9 inches. The special feature is of course the very narrow doorway.

COTTARS' HOUSES, SCARINISH.

STONE CIRCLE, HOGH.

CHAPTER XII

TIREE—SANDHILL DWELLINGS

OF this class some fine specimens exist in Tiree, and indeed the more definite list may be prefaced by the remark that (as in Coll, but here to an even greater extent) in almost any part of the island where the soil is sandy and the surface has become broken, fragments of old unglazed pottery are to be found. Perhaps in Tiree especially, where the manufacture of home-made pots (or 'craggans') has only ceased within a very few years (twenty at the most), much cannot be made of this feature as an argument in favour of the antiquity of these sites.

Within the village of Scarinish itself, in a sandhill north of the harbour and distant from it only a stone's-throw, are to be found occasional flaked flints, together with fragments of pottery of precisely the same description as those upon the more remote sandhills with undoubted ancient sites of dwellings, or unearthed from the kitchen-middens of the Duns.

In Scarinish, at a deep break in the grass-grown sandbank adjoining the east side of the road which runs northwards to Gott Bay, was seen a six-inch layer of ashes and periwinkle shells. This may not be a very ancient kitchen-midden, especially as fragments of lime and glass occur, and there are also two other similar layers upon the opposite edge of the roadway, consisting at that part chiefly of the shells of limpets and periwinkles, with coal ashes —thus evidently of modern origin—and we were informed that a cottar's house stood close to the latter point within the past fifty years.

Near Ruaig, at the east end of Gott Bay, some pottery was found, with a hammer-stone and a single flint. Close to the hamlet of Vaul, half a mile north-west of Ruaig and at the west end of Traigh Bhalla, in a small patch of broken turf were two hammer-stones and fragments of pottery, including two pieces patterned. Here is a small kitchen-midden, and not far from it another much larger one with pottery and many shells.

Upon the sand slopes above the beach at the centre of Vaul Bay is a distinct kitchen-midden with shells, and near it some flints and hammer-stones with a little pottery, two bits showing simple patterns. Again, in a similar position at Salum Bay (immediately to the east of Vaul), were many flints and some well-marked hammer-stones.

Close to the west of Baugh, at Port Eibrig, just below Cnoc Eibrig (already suggested as a possible Dun site, and not to be confounded with Cnoc Ibrig or Dun Ibrig, which are respectively about a mile and half a mile to the north-east), were fragments of flint and a little pottery.

The first of the four extensive sandhills of Tiree,—each covering an area ranging from several to very many acres, and which, from the remains, seem rightly to be associated with groups of ancient dwellings,—is at CORNAIG, a low-lying and comparatively level tract, close to the north end of Loch Bhasapol, and including the entire space—nearly half a mile—between that loch and the shore. On its west side is Crois or Kilmoluag, the site of one of the ancient chapels afterwards to be noticed. Pottery, flints, and bones are to be found over almost the whole area. At the north is a kitchen-midden with horses' teeth and bones, a few flints and a very little pottery. Midway, approaching Loch Bhasapol, were found more flints and pottery, and a large number of leg-bones of horses, a curious feature being that many of these lay to-gether in two separate heaps. Still farther south, pottery became more plentiful, including one piece with pattern, and another which seemed to be part of a small cup. An interest-ing feature is a large mound of ashes in successive strata, black upon red—these latter being quite ferruginous and evidently the refuse from a forge. At Cornaig only a few hammer-stones were to be seen—none of them to be classed as good specimens—as also two bone pins.

Passing over, for the meantime, the very large sandbank of Balamhuilinn (nearly a mile west from Cornaig), which is fully noticed in the next chapter among prehistoric burial-sites although also containing several small kitchen-middens, our next locality is at KILKENNETH, immediately around the ruined chapel which still exists there. Within a short radius to the east of the chapel are a number of kitchen-middens with hearths and ashes, shells, teeth and bones of the horse, together with other bones, although periwinkle and limpet shells predominate.

At this part flints and hammer-stones are decidedly scarce, while pottery, though abundant, is very coarse and rarely patterned. One hearth was observed to consist of small pebbles laid upon much larger. These facts would seem to point to a comparatively more recent occupation of the sites eastward from Kilkenneth chapel.

Towards the north-east, pottery was especially plentiful, including large fragments and others with some elaboration of shape by way of ogee curves, as also a few with patterns. One very thick piece, in coarse clay, evidently formed part of the pedestal of a large ornamental vessel.

To the extreme north, some 300 yards from the chapel and near the fence of Hogh farm, is a group of about thirty small cairns with ashes, some kitchen-middens, and much coarse pottery—these cairns being evidently the sites of ancient hearths.

In the opposite or southerly direction, pottery is quite rare except some of a particularly rude nature at two large kitchen-middens,—with limpet shells, bones, ashes, and hammer-stones,—three or four hundred yards south of the chapel. Indeed the intervening ground immediately south of the latter seems to have been used for pagan burials, and near the sea, half a mile west, there is the appearance of a prehistoric cemetery, with hammer-stones and flints in some quantity, but very little pottery—thus differing entirely from the eastward characteristics, as is afterwards noticed in connection with ancient burial sites.

Two complete jars have within recent years been discovered at Kilkenneth, one of them of the domestic type, although the other can only be mentioned from hearsay, as having been found east of the chapel, and containing some obliterated coins. Towards the south and east occurs a little corroded iron, including fragments of large cast-iron pots, which cannot be classed as ancient.

At BALAMEANACH (literally 'Middle-town,' by which name, or rather 'Middleton,' the houses at its northern extremity are now known) nearly two miles south of Kilkenneth, and between Cnoc a' Claodh (once a Christian burying-ground, see *postea*) and the large dyke which cuts off Kenavara headland on the south, are other ancient sites, although those next Cnoc a' Claodh appear to have been pagan burials. Near the Kenavara boundary a kitchen-midden is to be seen—a thick layer of limpet-shells and bones; and on the west is to be found another. In both places a few hammer-stones occur, but very little in the way of pottery or flints. Still farther west upon Barrapol[1]—really only a continuation of Balameanach—were more hammer-stones, a little pottery and flint, and a piece of iron slag.

It will be observed that each of these three sites—Cornaig, Kilkenneth, and Balameanach—is associated with that of an ancient Christian chapel. This fact is noteworthy, and may suggest a presumption that the Sandhills were occupied as dwelling-places before the period of erection of the chapels. Indeed the peculiar characteristics of objects found upon the

---

[1] An annular brass brooch (with simulated black-letter inscription), found at Barrapol, is figured in the *Proc. Soc. Antiq. Scot.*, vol. xix. p. 13 (1885).

Sandhills, in so far as they differ from those in the Duns, point
to a greater antiquity for the former, even if it be conceded—
as it must—that their occupation has also continued beyond that
of the Duns, probably even to so recent a date as about the end of
the seventeenth century.   The special characteristics to which reference is here made, are first, the abundance of flint ; and second,
the different stamp of patterned pottery, which is distinguished
both by its thinner and in a way coarser nature, and by the
crudeness and simplicity of the designs shown.   So much is
this the case (as has been said in regard to Coll) that without
knowing whence a specimen comes, it is usually easy at a glance
to tell whether it is from a Dun or Sandhill.   This remark
does not apply to the thick unpatterned pottery, most of
which is very similar wherever found.

The last of the four larger Sandhill groups of dwellings in
Tiree is above the shore of TRAIGH BHEIDHE (pronounced 'Tra
Vee'), immediately to the west of Balaphuil village, distant not
a mile south-east from Balameanach and Barrapol, and about a
mile north-east from Temple-Patrick.   Of all four Sandhill sites,
this shows most signs of a comparatively recent occupation.[1]
Next the Balaphuil end were noticed four or five kitchen-midden
mounds with ashes, bones (chiefly of fish), shells (mussels,
periwinkles, and limpets), a little pottery (one piece patterned), and
some iron including a large fish-hook, much corroded.   Westwards

---

[1] The kitchen-midden nearest Balaphuil is very large, and about 4 feet thick. This
is a most interesting site, although it contains, in addition to old pottery, glass and glazed
ware of modern types.

the character changes, and here were numerous flints (some of them scrapers) and bones of animals (including horses' teeth), but no kitchen-middens or pottery. Over the whole area not one satisfactory hammer-stone could be found, although a few poor specimens were seen.

As found upon the Sandhills of Tiree (but whether to be associated with dwellings or burials cannot be stated), mention must here be made of two remarkable bronze specimens obtained in 1897 by Lord Archibald Campbell, who kindly gave the writer an opportunity of examining them. One of these is a most peculiar pin about three inches in length with a semi-spherical fluted head, curved on the top but flat below. The special feature, however, is that the pin itself is of hybrid form, being *round* in the upper half and *square* in the lower, coming there to a sharp point, the whole thoroughly polished. The other object is evidently a netting-needle, of similar length, with an oblong hammered head and a tiny hook at the point. An oval stone axe, three and a quarter inches long with a half-inch hole perforated through its centre, has been found on Ben Hynish in Tiree; as also (locality unknown) a two-inch pin of bronze wire, its head projecting about a quarter of an inch to one side at a right angle, this bend being strengthened and ornamented by two flat circular twists given to the wire, making thus a loop or eye.

CHAPTER XIII

TIREE—PREHISTORIC BURIAL-SITES

FOUR stone circles still exist in Tiree, and we were told of two others, formerly to be seen between Ben Gott and Balaphetrish, but could find no trace of either, the stones of one indeed having been removed for building purposes.

The two largest of the four remaining examples occur as a pair of circles close to the north-west of the township of Moss, and fully half a mile south-east from Hogh farm-house. Both of them are of considerable area, and of the regular type, which (as regards Scotland at least) has been usually found when excavated to contain burials of the bronze age. Only a very few of the pillar-stones now stand erect, and close to the southmost of these two circles, at the centre of its east side, is a very distinct mound. The two other circles are upon boggy land between Poll Odhras-gair and Ben Gott, within half a mile to the east of the first named. These are much smaller—each only about 26 yards in diameter—but appear to be otherwise of the same type, with the addition that they show indications of ancient burials. The first contains in its centre a slight unshapely mound, and the second has in a like position four large stones arranged as if forming two sides of a cist, although of a very unusual size. It may be noted that each of these two minor circles stands about a hundred yards east from a small loch—of which the names are respectively Loch a' Bhleoghan and Loch a' Chapuil.

Near the north end of Tiree, about 150 yards south of Dun Beg a' Chaolais, is a small circular stone dyke upon the summit of a rocky knoll, which appeared to the writer as not unlikely to have been a burial-site.

A little to the north of Loch na Buaile (with its island Dun) is a slight walled enclosure about 12 yards in diameter and containing a cairn near its southern end.

At Crossapol, between the road and the beach, is a small erection of only about 3 feet interior diameter upon the centre of a distinct artificial mound. Its size, of course, precludes any idea of this having been a dwelling, nor does it appear to have been a mere shieling.

Upon the shore, at Port na Luinge, immediately to the east of Soroby churchyard, is the traditional site of an ancient pagan cemetery. Here were still to be found a little pottery, a few bones, and some horses' teeth, as also two hammer-stones, thus far attesting its reputed character. It is said that about twenty years ago, in the course of formation of the road which lies between this place and the churchyard, several cists containing complete urns were discovered.[1]

In this class, however, the Sandhill sites are perhaps of most

---

[1] *Proc. Soc. Antiq. Scot.*, vol. xvi. p. 463 ; and also from oral testimony. Other stone cists of the ordinary type, and presumptively of pagan origin, have occasionally been found in Tiree, but none of these was to be seen in an undamaged state.

interest, and they certainly present the greatest difficulties in the way of explanation.

At BALAMHUILINN, above the strand of the same name and a mile west from Cornaig, is an immense tract of blown sand. This covers an area of more than 150 acres, extending westwards to Dun Beannaig and the shore, being bounded on the north by small sea-cliffs, and sloping south to a level near the burn named Abhuinn Ban.

From the loose and shifting nature of the sandy surface (which indeed seemed to have changed materially at each of six or more successive visits from 1897 to 1901) it is difficult, if not impossible, to give any accurate description of the ancient remains occurring here and there in this most interesting site. To the north there has been a walled enclosure, of irregularly rectangular shape, its limits being clearly defined towards the north-west and north (beyond a group of massive rocks outcropping through the sand) as following the outline of the cliffs, at first south to north and then west to east (the ruined wall showing distinctly both of these portions), while towards the south and east are other boundaries of stones in regular line, although sometimes only intermittently through the sands. Within this enclosure—as over almost the whole of the Balamhuilinn site—the drifting sand is so deep as to make the scarcity of relics not surprising. A good many bones (including a number of horses' teeth) were seen, as also a few flints and fragments of pottery. Several hammer-stones, an iron nail or rivet, and a large brass pin of comparatively modern type, were also noticed. The only really valuable find

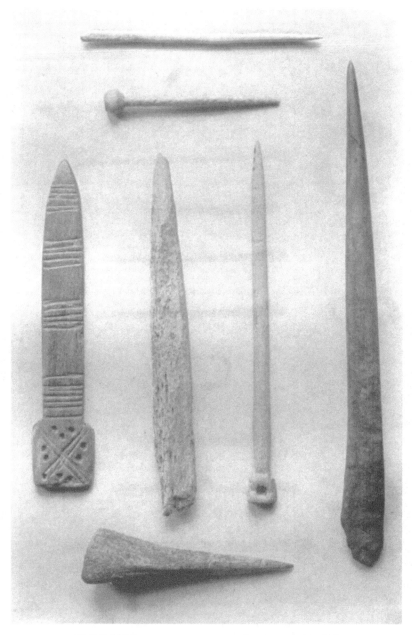

BONE PINS, ETC., ACTUAL SIZE. (SEE ALSO PP. 39, 42.)

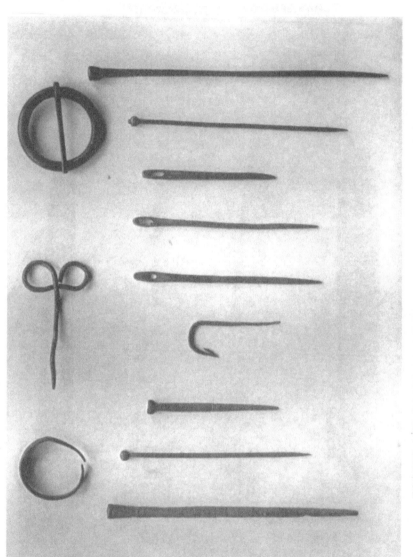

BRONZE AND BRASS ARTICLES, ACTUAL SIZE. (SEE ALSO PP. 3, 38, 138, 155.)

was a remarkable bone pin, measuring three and a half inches by half an inch, thin, and with flat sides.   From its shape, one may judge it to have been an ornament for the hair.   The head is nearly three-quarters of an inch square with a St. Andrew's Cross incised upon each side, and there are four groups of parallel lines across the front of its stem—(see illustration facing p. 132).

In the same place, towards its west edge, it seemed strange to find three pieces of Balaphetrish 'marble,'—a pink stone with greenish spots—which is only known (as to Tiree and a much wider area) to occur in a quarry at Balaphetrish, midway between the Dun and the farmhouse, at a distance of over four miles from Balamhuilinn.

Still farther west, upon a wide outer ledge of rock above the shore, were some pieces of patterned pottery (of the sandhill type) together with a few flints and horses' teeth.   This is within about 200 yards to the north-east of Dun Beannaig, which is also upon the border of the sandhill, and here, immediately to the east of the Dun, upon the slope which descends towards it, was found another piece of patterned pottery, with flint-chips.

From near Dun Beannaig are the foundations of a long wall stretching eastwards across the Balamhuilinn sandhills, dotted at such close intervals by a number of cairns, that it may be described as resembling a wall of cairns.   This seems to have formed the northern boundary of a second enclosure, and there are also, towards the south-east and south, at least two other similar walls with cairns.   Within this second ruined fence are again numerous outcropping rocks, amongst and upon which are many small groups of stones which might be taken to indicate ancient burials. These sites are at least so circumscribed as to render it quite clear that they can never have been dwellings. Many bones were scattered about, with a few flints (only one scraper), hammer-stones, and some seals' teeth. A small piece of wrought metal was also found, somewhat in the shape of an 'S,' which may possibly have formed part of a horse's bit.

Towards the extreme south of these enclosures are two distinct kitchen-middens chiefly composed of limpets and periwinkles.

Farther south are a number of separate cairns, and another kitchen-midden not so well defined. No pottery whatever was to be seen near these sites, but a large quantity of horses' bones and teeth and several bone pins of manifestly artificial shape. These latter were distinctly associated with individual cairns, four pins lying close together upon one mound amidst other bones (evidently human), while upon another neighbouring and similar heap lay a hammer-stone and some horses' teeth.

Pottery is uncommon at the north end of Balamhuilinn, and apparently absent in the middle portion. Towards the south end—a comparatively level tract—are other isolated cairns and two very large mounds of loose sand, the whole surface strewn with occasional bones, potsherds, and flints, almost to the small stream Abhuinn Ban on the south-west, the character of the remains indicating the whole area of these extensive sandhills to have been used here and there for burials, in all probability co-eval with the occupation of the three neighbouring forts—Dun Beannaig, Dun Boråige Mor, and Dun Boraige Beg. Near the south end is a kitchen-midden of shells, bones, and pottery, a little south of a large irregularly-shaped hillock, with the remains of a connecting wall or causeway. Upon the west edge of this mound, at a recent visit, there lay upon the drifting sand (within a small rectangular stone cist, about 2 feet square) several human bones, and a skull containing four good back-teeth ; while, towards the opposite or eastern end, were kitchen-midden shells and bones, with several cairns of water-worn pebbles near the base.

A little to the north is another and much larger sand-heap of regular oval shape.[1] Here, in the summer of 1901, disclosed by the continual drift near its western end, were still more numerous human remains, including fragments of at least two or three different skulls, two jawbones, and also the practically complete skeleton of a child, laid with its feet to the south.

Between these two large mounds extend the remains of either a wall or a rough pavement, while towards the west are a number of isolated cairns strewn with bones (probably both human and of animals), and some flints. Here were also found several fragments of iron, one piece riveted into a very large isolated stone.

[1] This particular mound seems to have been at one period a Viking burial. In the original *Statistical Account*, vol. x. p. 402, it is stated that in a stackyard at Cornaig-beg (a mile east of Balamhuilinn) 'in digging pits in sandy ground, . . . there were found at different times human skeletons, and nigh them the skeletons of horses. They seemed to have been completely armed, according to the times.'

At Balamhuilinn was found a good smoothing-stone.[1]   Bones and teeth of the horse were of common occurrence throughout.

The KILKENNETH sandhills (of which the eastward portion has already been described in respect to dwellings) are very extensive, and present almost as much difficulty as Balamhuilinn in the attempt to classify them.   Indeed, upon a visit in July 1901, great changes were noticeable as compared with the years 1897 to 1899, grass prevailing much over the former bare sand (except towards the extreme east), so that features which had been previously quite distinct were then scarcely traceable.

Kilkenneth lies about two miles south-west of Balamhuilinn, and half a mile west from the ancient chapel, near the shore, is a large level tract bounded upon the east by a steep sandy slope, which has probably been an ancient raised beach.   Here flints and hammer-stones are much more plentiful than at the kitchen-midden sites around Kilkenneth Chapel (where both of these classes are scarcely observable), while on the other hand pottery is rarer, diminishing greatly towards the shore.

On the slope just mentioned a very little pottery was to be seen, with flints, some hammer-stones, horses' teeth, and also

---

[1] From the same general site were purchased the following articles :—

    A silver coin of Queen Elizabeth.

    A short needle (apparently of bronze) and a longer one of brass, both with large eyes.

    A bronze fish-hook.

    Four pins with coiled wire heads, apparently of brass.

The writer has also seen another bronze pin which was found at Balamhuilinn.   It measured about $2\frac{1}{2}$ inches in length, and had a large round head marked with longitudinal grooves.

many seals' teeth, and a few rude bone pins—both of these latter occurring in groups of several at a time.

Upon the flat, farther west, are the remains of numerous small cairns, some of them connected by walls or causeways in a row north and south, with occasional flints, hammer-stones, and fragments of pottery, two of these bearing the sandhill type of pattern. Here in 1897 (again in 1899 and 1901 to a less extent) the greater portion of a human skeleton was seen protruding through the sand with many other bones, especially those of horses, in the vicinity. Indeed there is every indication that this was an ancient burial-site, presumably of the Viking period.[1] Part of a deer's horn was also found with a distinct transverse cut across one end.

From this flat area the broken sands continue towards the north and south, but in both directions interspersed by frequent sand-heaps covered with bents. To the north, ancient sites are traceable at intervals until within a quarter of a mile of Dun Hanais, although relics are scarce. To the extreme south, near Traigh Ghrianal, about two hundred yards south of the level tract, is a large artificial erection—possibly a chambered cairn. This is now quite 12 feet high and 18 feet in diameter across the summit, where some very large stones lie near the edge, flush with the surface. The mound is strewn with stones; a few flints and bones here occur, together with some doubtful hammer-stones, but not a scrap of pottery was found upon three several visits.

[1] The bones and teeth of horses are here particularly common.

Between the sandy slope and the west of Kilkenneth Chapel is an intermediate space, much occupied by jutting rocks, amongst which are old hearths, kitchen-middens (with bones and shells), hammer-stones, and pottery, but little if any flint. Among the rocks were noticed on our first visit (of 1897) several distinct groups of small white (quartz) stones, although upon subsequent occasions these could not be verified. A cart-track leads seaward south of all the sites above mentioned (the chambered cairn only excepted), and upon its north side were found half a dozen good hammer-stones lying close together. Upon both edges of this roadway (but especially to its south) flaked flints are exceedingly plentiful,[1] more so indeed than at any other site known to the writer.

Some forty yards to the south of Kilkenneth Chapel, in a place where the absence of visible kitchen-middens or pottery is noteworthy, are the remains of a small square erection, perhaps a cist, formed of four stones and measuring some 2 feet across the interior.

Quite near this are traces of another enclosure, partly surrounded by one course of very large stones, lying east and west and apparently having contained a space of about 6 feet by 18 inches.

Small bronze brooches of about an inch in diameter, some with long and others with short pins, are occasionally found at Kilkenneth; one of these was given to the writer by Dr. Buchanan.

---

[1] A pocketful could be gathered in a very few minutes.

SITE OF (?) BURIAL CAIRN, BALAMEANACH.

SOROBY CROSS, WEST SIDE.

SOROBY CROSS, EAST SIDE.

At BALAMEANACH (a mile and a half south of Kilkenneth Chapel, and just south of another old Christian burial-ground, Cnoc a' Claodh) was to be seen the greater portion of a horse's skeleton, with some fragments of pottery, only one bit patterned. Hammer-stones and flints are here quite scarce.   Towards the south end, not far from the Kenavara boundary wall, and near the large kitchen-midden already noticed (among Sandhill dwellings, p. 127), is a most remarkable site—a level circle of about 12 yards in diameter, closely strewn with small stones (most of them broken), and containing in its centre another circle of 48 inches across, regularly paved with rounded quartz pebbles [1] of comparatively large size, these again carefully edged with still larger ordinary water-worn stones, the whole evidently *in situ* as when laid.   This we can only conclude to have been a burial-cairn, now completely ruined, and with merely the base remaining (see

---

[1] This fact, together with other groups of these pebbles found at Kilkenneth, as noted on page 138, opens up an interesting field of research. Sir Arthur Mitchell, K.C.B., LL.D., in a paper contributed to the *Proc. Soc. Antiq. Scot.*, vol. xviii. p. 286, discusses the occurrence of white quartz stones in chambered cairns (burials) and cists of pagan times, and also mentions, from his personal observation, similar pebbles laid upon no fewer than eight graves in the churchyard of Kilmalew near Inveraray. The present writer (before seeing Sir Arthur's paper) was much struck by finding, in 1898, two small groups of these pebbles heaped against headstones in Keills churchyard, North Knapdale,—one of the tombstones dated 1841, within the ancient ruined church itself, and the other (undated) in the surrounding graveyard which is still used for burials. He also specially noted the existence of another similar—but larger—collection of quartz stones upon the top of a low ruined erection (said to be St. Cormac's tomb) immediately to the east of the sculptured cross upon Eilean Mor in Knapdale.

Here may be added a parallel reference (from the *Graphic* of October 1898, describing the battle of Omdurman in the Soudan) to a ' custom of Mahomedans all over the world, to place white pebbles on burial-grounds.'

illustration).   Hardly any pottery is to be observed near this spot.

Upon the Barrapol portion of the same sandhills, west of Loch a' Phuil, was found another horse's skeleton, and somewhat to the south a few flints and good hammer-stones and a piece of iron-slag, as has already been mentioned in connection with the sandhill dwelling-sites.

There yet remains to be noticed a series of mounds, evidently of considerable antiquity, at EARNAL, a large and comparatively level common,[1] adjoining the north end of Loch Riaghain, and nearly a mile west from the old chapels at Kirkapol.   Within a quarter of a mile of this loch (chiefly between the Vaul and Balaphetrish fences, but several of them on the Balaphetrish side) are about twenty long low mounds.   These all lie approximately north and south, and are usually only about 3 feet in height. One much larger is about 6 feet high and 80 feet long, broadest at its south end and tapering towards the north, which latter form is indeed characteristic of the whole group.   In the same vicinity, upon the top of a small hill called Cnoc Earnal within sight of the island Dun on Loch na Gile, is a still larger mound somewhat curved and about 90 feet in length.

[1] This probably formed part of 'The Wyle,' which has been mentioned in Chapter x. in connection with the supposed Dun upon Cnoc Creagach.

CHAPTER XIV

TIREE—PRE-REFORMATION CHAPELS AND BURIAL-GROUNDS

DR. REEVES' Monograph upon the ecclesiastical antiquities of Tiree has already been cited in regard to the very brief notice which it also includes of the same class of sites in Coll. Before taking up his list of thirteen ancient chapels in Tiree, a few quotations may be given as to the island's general ecclesiastical history, so closely interwoven with that of Iona.

Dr. Reeves, who remains the best authority upon this subject, completely identifies Tiree with the *Ethica insula* or *Ethica terra* of Adamnan, and the *terra, insula,* or *regio, Hyth,* or *Hith* of the Irish chronicles.[1] St. Columba, soon after his coming to Iona in A.D. 563, founded 'in terra Heth' a monastery or penitential

---

[1] Reeves' *Adamnan*, p. 48. To the name of Tiree have been ascribed only too numerous derivations. In the Icelandic Sagas it takes the form of *Tyrvist*—*vist* being explained as signifying an abode or dwelling. The old *Statistical Account* gives *Tir-i* or 'the land of Iona,' and the *New Statistical Account* (p. 195) has its variant of *Tir-reidh*, 'the flat or level land,' perhaps with some allusion to 'The Reef,' a large plain near the middle of the island, and believed to have been at one time covered by the sea. Dr. Reeves' (*Monograph*, p. 237) gives *Tir-Aodha* pronounced *Tir-Ee*—the land of Hugh—as an Irish explanation. On the other hand, the native pronunciation is said now to be (phonetically) 'Tchirooch,' and to mean 'the land of food.' Where so many authorities differ, it would be presumptuous to express an opinion. Blaeu's map of 1662 has the spelling 'Tyrryf'; while Reeves' *mdamnan*, p. 48, gives the varying forms of *Tirieth* (12th century), *Tyre-è* (Fordun),

house, 'Campus navis, id est Mag-lunga vocatur,' over which pre-
sided St. Baithene, his own first-cousin (and immediate successor),
being also one of the twelve disciples who originally accompanied
him to Iona.[1] It is also recorded that Columbanus (*Colmanellus*
of the Irish calendar, patron-saint of Kilcolmonell in Argyllshire
and of Colmonell in Ayrshire) sailed from Ireland to the island
of *Hyth*, and after there receiving ordination at the hands of
St. Columba, returned to his own country.[2]

There must indeed have been a very frequent communication
between Ireland and Tiree during the sixth century, and without
doubt the local dedications in this island to Saints Kenneth[3]
(Cainnech, Canice, or Choinnich), Bride (Brigid), Finnian, Moluoc,

Tyriad (1343), *Tereyd* (1354), *Tyriage* (1390), *Tiereig* (1496), until it has been reduced to
the present form of *Tiree*, or often *Tyree*.

One extract from the *Annals of Ulster*, anno 678 (quoted in Reeves' *Adamnan*, p. 376),
'Interfectio Generis Loairnn in Tir-inn, *i.e.* Ferchair Fada, et Britones victores erant,'
seems certainly to refer to Tiree, the more especially when taken in conjunction with other
notices of Ferchar Fada, to whom, as successor, A.D. 689, to Maelduin in the kingdom of
Scottish Dalriada, the sceptre passed from the house of Gabhran to that of Loarn. This
Ferchar Fada was ancestor of the MacQuarries and MacKinnons, two important clans in
Iona and Tiree (*Ibid.*, pp. 203, 437).

[1] Reeves' *Adamnan*, pp. 59, 245. St. Columba died at Iona, June A.D. 597.

[2] *Ibid.*, pp. 29, 125 ; also Reeves' *Monograph*, p. 234.

[3] St. Kenneth is said to have lived for some time in Tiree (*Heth*) (Skene's *Celtic Scotland*,
second edn., vol. ii. p. 132). Probably about the same period (certainly not later than A.D. 577,
when St. Brendan died) we read that four founders of monasteries (the two above named,
together with St. Brendan and Cormac) came from Ireland and visited St. Columba in the
island of Hinba, which was evidently Eilean na Naomh, one of the Garveloch group (Reeves'
Adamnan, p. 220). Further, about the year A.D. 565, St. Columba, accompanied by
St. Kenneth and St. Comgall, ventured upon a mission to the fort (identified by Dr. Reeves
with Craig Phadrick near Inverness) of the Pictish King, Brude, whom they succeeded in
converting to Christianity (*Ibid.*, pp. 150-152). St. Kenneth was born in 517, and died in
600 (*Ibid.*, p. 121).

Oran, and Patrick, are due to this cause.   Dr. Reeves quotes from the *Life of St. Kenneth of Aghaboe* that a certain layman named Tulchan journeyed from Ireland to the island of *Hithe*, where he became a monk.[1]   He also mentions St. Comgall, who had founded the monastery of Bangor in Ulster, A.D. 558, as sailing to Britain and founding another at a certain village 'in regione Heth' under date A.D. 565 ;[2] and tells how St. Brendan (founder of Clonfert in A.D. 559) first built a monastery called *Ailech* upon the mainland (*i.e. Scotland*), and afterwards at another place 'in regione Heth' a church and village.[3]

Findchan, also a contemporary of St. Columba, founded the monastery of *Artchain* 'in Ethica terra,'[4] about A.D. 565.

Dr. Reeves, in his *Monograph*, proceeds thus to enumerate the ancient ecclesiastical remains in Tiree, the attached numbers following no geographical sequence, but being merely adopted, for convenience, from his own arrangement.

SOROBY.—This was at Port na Luinge on the south-east   +I

---

[1] Reeves' *Monograph*, p. 235. The same Tulchan was the father of St. Munna (also known as St. Fintan).   From this saint, who came to Iona in 597, just after St. Columba's death, the Scottish *Kilmun* derives its name, and near Ballachulish (on an island in Loch Leven) was another chapel dedicated to St. Mund (Reeves' *Adamnan*, pp. 20-22, 372).

[2] *Ibid.*, p. 220, also *Monograph*, pp. 235, 236.   He died A.D. 602.

[3] Reeves' *Monograph*, p. 236.   St. Brendan died in 577, aged 95, and is patron saint of Kilbrandon in the island of Seil (Reeves' *Adamnan*, pp. lxxiv and 222).

[4] *Ibid.*, pp. 66, 370.   But compare this with *Ibid.*, p. 21, where it is noted that St. Fintan or Munna was the founder of a church at '*Ath-caoin* in the island of Coimrighi, at *Achadh-leicce*,' these names which we place in italics being curiously like *Artchain* and *Ailech*, above attributed to Findchan and St. Brendan respectively.   *Artchain* seems to agree with Ardkirknish, near Balaphetrish in Tiree—the *Ard chircnis* of the Ordnance Survey map.

shore of the island, and immediately to the north of Balamartin township.   It is certainly the *Campus Lunge* of Adamnan, as also the *Campus navis* or *Magh-Luinge* of the Irish chronicles,[1] and, as has already been noted, was a monastery founded by St. Columba, and in his time ruled by St. Baithene as *præpositus* or prior.

Of the Chapel[2] there remain only the very faintest traces (although we were informed that the foundations show distinctly below the surface) near the north-west corner of Soroby church-yard, one of the three burying-grounds still in use in Tiree, the other two almost adjoining each other at Kirkapol.

In Soroby churchyard stands a massive bossed stone cross, measuring 32 inches in extreme width, and 46 inches in height above the soil.   Here also at least six ancient grave-slabs of the West Highland type (with two eighteenth-century table-stones) still remain.   By far the most interesting of the monu-ments here, however, is one which measures about 74 inches in length by 9 inches in breadth at the head and 13 inches at the foot.   Unfortunately the stone is broken right through some

---

[1] Reeves, in his *Monograph*, p. 240, and in *Adamnan*, p. 59, quotes an Irish reference to *Sancta Brigida de Mag-luinge*, and identifies this saint as the patroness of Kilbride Chapel, next to be noted—*postea*, No. II.   There are two later references to this monastery in the Irish Annals—first in A.D. 673, where Tighernach records its destruction by fire ; and second, in the *Annals of the Four Masters*, A.D. 770, where is entered the obit of *Conall Abb Maighe Luinge*, *i.e.* 'Conall abbot of Magh Luing' (*Ibid.*).

[2] As to the monasteries, chapels, and cells of St. Columba's time, it is supposed that they were originally constructed of wood or wattles and clay ; or that, when built of stone, they were of the character of beehive-cells (Fowler's *Adamnan*, pp. xxxviii and xxxix.   *Reed-*thatching seems to have been in use, *Ibid.*, p. 113).

CROSS OF ST. MICHAEL THE ARCHANGEL, SOROBY.

(REDUCED FROM A RUBBING.)

ROCK CHAPEL AT KIRKAPOL (?ST. COLUMBA'S).

19 inches from the smaller end; the very top is also slightly damaged, but the sides are sharp and clear throughout. In the upper part it bears in strong relief a representation of St. Michael and the Dragon, and near the other end the figure of Death holding by the hand a female ecclesiastic. Between these groups runs the inscription, in raised Gothic characters[1] :—

> Hic est crux
> Michae(lis) ar
> changeli dei
> Anna prior
> isa de P

The two table-stones are to MacLeans, and bear the family arms. One of them has the name of Mr. Hector MacLean, minister of Coll, and is apparently in memory of his son.

Within a square enclosure of the Macarthurs, near the south-east corner of the churchyard, are fragments of a slab and a cross of the West Highland type, utilised as head-stones. One of these bears foliage ornament upon both sides, and a groove down the edges; the other is a broken cross, the arms still partly remaining and the back rough. In about the centre of the older portion of the churchyard (which has been very recently enlarged to the south) is a rectangular head-stone bearing in its centre a cross pattée upon one side, the other being blank.

---

[1] Dr. Reeves erroneously inserts *soror* before *Anna*, and substitutes *abbatissa* for *priorisa*. The slab is supposed by him to have been a memorial or votive cross erected during the incumbency of Anna, but afterwards carried away to Tiree. He also states that the tombstone of Prioress Anna, who died in 1543, still remained (1852) within the nunnery of Iona (*Monograph*, p. 239).

+II   The chapel of KILBRIDE,[1] of which absolutely nothing is now to be seen, was in Cornaig-Mor, a quarter of a mile south of the corn-mill, and about the same distance east from Loch Bhasapol. Mention has already been made of this chapel as dedicated to St. Brigid of Magh-Luing. She was one of thirteen saints of the same name.[1]

The burying-ground is locally stated to have been upon the site of the present stackyard of *Lag na Cruach*, the 'hollow of the heaps,' and Dr. Reeves gives (p. 241) the following description : 'It is on the north side, in the farm of Cornagmore, and human remains[2] which are found here indicate a cemetery where a small chapel is known to have existed, the walls of which were removed to help in building some ancient cabins.'

Rock crops out within this stackyard, and in its centre lies a hollowed stone about 2 feet long, which however may have been a mortar in which to pound grain, and not a font.

+III   Concerning the monastery of ARTCHAIN, already mentioned as founded by Findchan[3] in Tiree, it is supposed that this name has passed into *Ardkirknish*, where, a little to the east of Bala-phetrish Hill, was formerly a chapel with its cemetery. On the

---

[1] Reeves' *Mònograph*, p. 240.

[2] The old *Statistical Account*, vol. x. p. 402, refers to human skeletons, weapons, and armour, and near to them, the skeletons of horses, as having been found in a stackyard at Cornaig-*beg*. If this be an error for Cornaig-*mor* (the two Cornaigs being contiguous) the site would fully agree with that of Kilbride churchyard, although the remains described are of a non-ecclesiastical character.

[3] Findchan's name is understood to appear in *Kilfinichen*, Mull. These very similar names in connection with Tiree (*Findchan* and *Fintan*, *antea* ; also two *Cill Fhinneins* upon the Ordnance map, although one is spelt *Fhinnean*, quite near each other—our

six-inch Ordnance Survey map this site is marked 'Ard chircnis' and 'Cill Fhinnein,' but the latter evidently in error, another (and from local nomenclature *the correct*) 'Cill Fhinnean' being situated at Kenovay near the west shore of Balaphetrish Bay, and a mile and a half from Ardkirknish.   At Ardkirknish there are no satisfactory traces of the old chapel, but immediately to the north of the rocks is a comparatively level plateau with what may be the foundations of an ancient ecclesiastical building placed east and west.   Or it may have been a little to the south, in a cleared space between the rocks and the road, where a few large blocks of stone stand erect as if part of a boundary of somewhat circular shape.

KILFINNIAN, in Kenovay, is within a quarter of a mile south +IV from the south-west corner of Balaphetrish Bay.   Here the outlines of the churchyard are still distinct, and the foundations of the chapel even more marked (towards the south of the enclosure), measuring 22 by $11\frac{1}{2}$ feet inside.   A spot was pointed out as the site of the latest burial some sixty years ago.

At KIRKAPOL, opposite the middle of Gott Bay, and a mile +V } and a half north of Scarinish, are three separate sites close +VI }

Nos. III. and IV.), give rise to great difficulties.   There were however two famous Irish saints of the same name, St. Finnian, one of Moville and the other of Clonard, under both of whom St. Columba studied (Reeves' *Adamnan*, p. 103).

A phrase which occurs in Adamnan's *Life of St. Columba* (Reeves' *Adamnan*, p. 207), with reference primarily to *Campus Lunge*, is somewhat striking.   It runs 'in ceteris ejusdem insulæ monasteriis,' thus inferring that there were in Tiree 'other' monasteries besides *Campus Lunge*, although the words are perhaps not to be taken *au pied de la lettre*. We have already noticed *Artchain*, while that said to have been founded 'in regione Heth' by St. Comgall would make a third.   *Three* monasteries indeed seem to have been a more than ample supply for the whole island.

together;—a very old chapel upon a rock and uninclosed; another mediæval church within its graveyard; and (nearest the shore), a burial-ground without any existing remains of a former chapel.

Of the two churches, that upon the isolated rock, about 100 yards to the north, is the smaller and also undoubtedly much the more ancient. This chapel measures outside 29 feet by 16 feet 6 inches, and inside 23 feet 6 inches by 11 feet 6 inches, leaving a thickness of about 30 inches for each of the walls.

Dr. Reeves remarks that as at Kilkenneth and Temple-Patrick (the only other very ancient chapels in Tiree of which more than the slightest foundations of the walls remain) this example has had no eastern window, but instead, two narrow deeply-splayed lancets in the chancel, through the north and south walls. Of these, that on the south is imperfect, but both have evidently been of the same size, viz., 22 by 7 inches outside, splayed to 31 by 25 inches at the interior. The round-headed doorway, on the south side near the west gable, is exceedingly narrow, measuring only 23½ inches across, and the floor is of the natural rock, with all its unevenness of surface. The gables and north side are almost entire, but in the south wall, immediately west from the splayed window (of which only the east half shows), occurs a large gap of more than 2 yards. Above this break, the upper portion of the masonry (some 2 feet in depth), still tenaciously remains in position, forming a rough arch, which however can scarcely thus hold out for more than a short time. Upon the exterior of the west gable is a recess (of triangular

TWO CHAPELS AT KIRKAPOL.

SLABS OF THE WEST HIGHLAND TYPE AT KIRKAPOL.

(FROM RUBBINGS,—SCALE, 1 IN 12.)

shape but flattened at the top), about 20 inches in height, which has apparently held an image. No name is given by tradition to this chapel, but from other evidence it seems to have been dedicated to St. Columba.[1] Certainly such has been the case either with this or with the larger and much later chapel next to be described in Claodh Beg.

The other existing chapel (evidently the most modern of this former group of three) stands a little to the south of the last mentioned, within a graveyard known as CLAODH BEG, meaning +V simply 'the little burying-ground.' This building is of much larger dimensions than the rock-chapel, its interior measuring 37 feet 3 inches by 17 feet 6 inches. In the west gable is a built-up, round-headed doorway, and high in the south wall are two narrow splayed windows, measuring 33 by 15 inches outside.[2] Within Claodh Beg are at least eight sculptured slabs of the West Highland type. Two of these are to the south of the

---

[1] Munch, in *The Chronicle of Man and the Sudreys*, pp. 186, 187, copies from the archives of the Vatican a document issued by Pope Gregory XI., dated at Pontemsorgia (near Avignon), 20th September 1375, and addressed to the Bishop of Lismore in favour of 'Ayg' MacPetri perpetui vicarij parrochialis ecclesie sancte Columbe de Kerepol Sodorensis diocesis.' The same writer previously states (p. 138) that in 1247 Argyll formed part of the *Diocesis Lismorensis*.

[2] Muir, in his *Characteristics of Old Church Architecture*, pp. 152, 153, assigns to this chapel a date not later than the thirteenth century, and describes (1861) a semi-circularly arched doorway 'on the south-west,'—that is, in the south wall,—in addition to the western door. There is now no doorway on the south, but a large gap appears in the place where it may have existed. There is also a still wider break in the east gable, so extensive indeed as to render it quite unsafe, even apart from a recently widened crack in the north wall adjoining. Very probably this east gable contained a window. Muir also figures a dedication Cross (of Latin form) in the west gable, but this was not now to be seen, owing perhaps to the thick harling upon the wall.

church ; one of them lies flat, broken across and much defaced ; the other stands erect and is evidently the upright shaft of a cross (the top broken off), about 36 inches in height above ground, 8 inches wide, and nearly 3 inches thick.   This latter has fluted grooves down its edges, and foliage ornament upon both sides. East of the chapel are six other slabs, some of them much overgrown by herbage in summer.   Upon two of the six the ornament is barely traceable, and of another stone only half remains ; the most distinct measures 68 by 15 inches, and is a really fine specimen, with a two-handed sword sculptured amidst foliage ornament on its face, and upon the bevelled edges (to north and west) the following incised lettering [1] :—

+𝔉𝔦𝔫𝔤𝔬𝔫𝔦𝔲𝔰 : 𝔓𝔯𝔦𝔬𝔯 : 𝔡𝔢 : 𝔜 : 𝔪𝔢 : 𝔡𝔢𝔡𝔦𝔡 :
𝔓𝔥𝔦𝔩𝔦𝔭𝔭𝔬 : 𝔍𝔬𝔥𝔞𝔫𝔫𝔦𝔰 : 𝔢𝔱 : 𝔰𝔲𝔦𝔰 : 𝔉𝔦𝔩𝔦𝔦𝔰 : 𝔄𝔫𝔫𝔬 :
𝔇𝔬𝔪𝔦𝔫𝔦 | m° cccc° rcb°.

[1] According to Reeves' *Monograph*, p. 241, ' This prior was of the Clann MacFinnguine, now called Mackinnon, and is thus noticed by MacFirbis :—" Finnguine, abbot of Hy, brother to Domhnall, son of Gillebride." '

In Stuart's *Sculptured Stones*, vol. ii., plate lxvi. (letterpress, p. 73), is shown the pedestal of a cross erected (presumably at St. Oran's Chapel, Iona, although not specifically located) in memory of the Abbot, and bearing as inscription :—

     + 𝔥𝔢𝔠 : 𝔢𝔰𝔱 : 𝔠𝔯𝔲𝔵 : 𝔉𝔦𝔫𝔤𝔬𝔫𝔦𝔦 : 𝔞𝔟𝔟𝔞𝔱𝔦
     𝔰 : 𝔢𝔱 𝔰𝔲𝔬𝔯𝔲𝔪 𝔣𝔦𝔩𝔦𝔬𝔯𝔲𝔪 : 𝔉𝔦𝔫𝔤𝔬𝔫𝔦𝔦 : 𝔢
     𝔱 𝔈𝔞𝔤𝔢.

This Abbot Fingonius (or another of the same name) is said to have died in 1500, and certainly in 1489 erected a cross (*Ibid.*, vol. ii., plate xlvii., letterpress, p. 27),—' +𝔥𝔢𝔠 : 𝔢𝔰𝔱 : 𝔠𝔯𝔲𝔵 : | 𝔏𝔞𝔠𝔠𝔩𝔞𝔫𝔫𝔦 : 𝔐𝔢𝔦𝔠 | : 𝔉𝔦𝔫𝔤𝔬𝔫𝔢 : 𝔢𝔱 : 𝔢𝔦𝔲𝔰 | : 𝔣𝔦𝔩𝔦𝔦 : 𝔍𝔬𝔥𝔞𝔫𝔫𝔦𝔰 : | 𝔄𝔟𝔟𝔞𝔱𝔦𝔰 : 𝔡𝔢 : 𝔜𝔭 | 𝔉𝔞𝔠𝔱𝔞 : 𝔞𝔫𝔫𝔬 : 𝔇𝔬𝔪𝔦 | 𝔫𝔦 : m.° cccc.° lrrr.° ir.° | '.

Attention may here be drawn to the names ' Eage ' of the pedestal inscription above noted, and ' Ayg' MacPetri' of the Papal Bull, dated 1375 and already quoted on p. 149. *Eage* and *Ayg'* evidently represent the Christian name *Hugh*, which also seems to be identical with *Aedh* and *Aidus* (Fowler's *Adamnan*, p. 176).

At a distance of some thirty yards to the south-east is a larger   +VI
cemetery known as CLAODH ODHRAIN, or *Claodh Mor*. This is
still in regular use as a burial-ground, and now contains no visible
traces of a chapel, although within the past few years a grave-
digger came upon what are evidently the foundations of one—
dedicated no doubt to St. Oran. Within this enclosure are two
slabs of the West Highland type, two much-defaced table-stones
(dating apparently from only the eighteenth century), and part of
the shaft and one arm of an old cross serving as a headstone,
perforated by a round hole close to its present top. Both of the
ancient slabs have foliage ornament, the more remarkable of the
two measuring 71 inches in length, and tapering in width from 17
to 14 inches. Near the top is the figure of a woman raising in
one hand a large loop, and holding a rod in the other. Immediately below (but inverted) are two animals, probably dogs, and
near the other end, a pair of shears. Below this again is represented a casket with metal mountings.

In Stuart's *Sculptured Stones*, vol. ii., plate lii., are figured
the fragments of a fine cross as then (*ca.* 1867) existing in this
burying-ground. 'On the shaft is a running pattern of foliage
and knot-work, and on one side a man on horseback at the
bottom. The upper part of the cross represents the Crucifixion on
one side, and a deer-hunt is on the other' (*Ibid.*, vol. ii. p. 29).
These fragments could not be found, and we were afterwards
informed that they had been removed to Inveraray Castle.

KILKENNETH. The dedication of this chapel was obviously to   +VII
St. Kenneth (the founder of Aghaboe monastery and from whom

Kilkenny takes its name). Indeed, from his companionship with St. Columba and their joint missionary visit to King Brude near Inverness,[1] it is evident that the two saints were intimate friends.

The walls of Kilkenneth Chapel are still in very complete preservation, with interior dimensions of 28 feet 9 inches by 13 feet 9 inches. Its northern and eastern walls are heaped outside by drifted sand nearly up to their summit, although the inside is almost clear. Immediately to the north-east corner is a rocky mound upon which lay many ancient human bones with at least one skull, although we were told that many such had been re-interred. In the west gable is a round-headed doorway about 27 inches wide, but imperfect on the south side. The only windows are two splayed lancets (9 inches wide outside, 24 inches inside), opposite to each other in the north and south walls, 33 inches from the east gable—that on the south being scarcely traceable.[2] The churchyard seems to have been confined to the section lying from the mid-north to the south-east, diverging from the chapel 44 feet and 37 feet at these extremes respectively, and here are the distinct remains of a wall, close to which was found one piece of flint evidently used as a core from which to strike flakes.

+VIII   KILMOLUAG, 'the church of St. Moluoc.' According to Dr. Reeves, 'This saint, who was the founder and patron of Lismore

---

[1] See p. 142, *antea*.

[2] Lord Archibald Campbell mentioned, as now in the possession of his family, a small bronze bell of only about two inches diameter, which was found some years ago at Kilkenneth.

KILKENNETH CHAPEL.

in Scotland, was a native of Ireland. . . . The stones of the old
chapel were employed to build the walls of cabins, and the space,
where the cemetery is shown to have been, is now in tillage.'[1]

This site, now quite undistinguishable, has been at Crois
(nearly half a mile north-west of Loch Bhasapol), where, upon
the six-inch Ordnance map are marked *A' Chrois* and close to
it, *Mullach na Croise*, though a more correct reading would seem
to be *Crois a' Moluag*.

TEMPLE-PATRICK is to the south of the considerable hill, Ben   +IX
Kenavara, and close to the south-west shore of Tiree. Towards
the east, between the hill-side and the sea, is a long narrow
space of comparatively level ground, and half a mile to the west,
surrounded by rocks, stands the Church of St. Patrick, now
reduced to its foundations and part of the east gable.[2]

Close to the chapel are two pillar-stones, one about 26 inches
high, incised upon each side with a Latin Cross, measuring
respectively 9¾ and 6 inches. The other, of coarser material,
is 38 inches long with similar crosses of 13¾ and 11½ inches
(see illustrations of both sides). Lying under the shadow of a
rock at the east gable was still another larger and ruder stone
of irregular shape and rough surface, its length varying from

---

[1] Reeves' *Monograph*, p. 242. St. Moluoc died A.D. 592 ; he was also known as Lugadius
or Lamluoc (Skene's *Celtic Scotland*, second edn., vol. ii. p. 133).

[2] The old *Stat. Acc.*, vol. x. p. 402, thus describes the condition of Temple-Patrick a
hundred years ago : 'The vestige of a wall incloses it in one-third of an acre of land. It is
26 by 11 feet within walls ; the side walls 5½ feet high ; one gable 6 inches thicker than
the other ; without a roof, and ill-built of stone and lime. A square altar at the east end
is still 18 inches high.' This description proves that serious dilapidation has occurred
within the past century.

42 to 36 inches.   Upon one side was a cross 16½ inches in length, with traces of a smaller one faintly cut below; while upon the reverse was a rude cross 11 inches long.   This would seem to be the stone to which Dr. Reeves refers,—'On the south there stands a pillar-stone with two crosses incised upon it, of which the lower is the more ancient.'[1]

The chapel walls seem to have been 3 feet thick, with the exception of the east gable, which is about 6 inches less.   This gable now measures at its greatest height 5½ feet inside and 7 feet outside, but is much broken towards both edges.   Upon a hillock about 10 yards to the north has been a separate oval-walled enclosure of about 6 by 3 yards, and here appear traces of an erection measuring 4 feet square inside.   Just below the chapel is a small well near the shore, and in the rocks at about high-water mark are several curious round and deep holes (but evidently natural), one of which is known as St. ·Patrick's Vat and has been described as 2 feet wide and 4 feet in depth.[2]

A little to the west are two stony beaches upon which are to be found the so-called 'Iona pebbles,'—water-worn fragments of serpentine rock.

+X   CNOC A' CLAODH, 'the hill of the burying-ground,' is a hillock close to the Barrapol side of the wire fence which divides that farm from Balameanach.   Indeed, this fence (quite a recent one) had to be deviated in the course of its erection, because of the human bones which were exhumed.   Such remains are

---

[1] Reeves' *Monograph*, p. 242.   [2] Old *Stat. Acc.*, vol. x. p. 402.

TEMPLE PATRICK, FROM NORTH

CROSSES AT TEMPLE PATRICK.

still to be seen here and there upon the surface. One hammer-stone was found, and about five years ago a bronze needle, with an eye very large in proportion, was picked up in the vicinity. Dr. Reeves describes the site as close to some cabins which were built from the walls of the chapel, but there seem now to be no cottages near.[1]

CLAODH BEG, 'the little burying-ground,' is perhaps in-   +XI
distinctly traceable upon the brow of the hill-side half a mile west from Hynish farm and about a hundred yards north-east of a large sheepfold. But, as mentioned by Dr. Reeves, this site is now quite effaced, although the name still survives.[2]

TEMPLEFIELD (now Todhar an Teampuill, 'the field (or fold)   +XII
of the church') is in Heylipol, south of the road to Barrapol, and half a mile south-west from Island House. Dr. Reeves states that it 'derived its name from a chapel, the site of which is now occupied by a school-house.' But since this was written (1852) the school has been in turn displaced by a manse of the Established Church. No ancient remains are now to be observed.

Lastly comes CROIS A' CHAOLAIS, of which burying-ground   +XIII
the very slightest traces still exist in a small enclosure behind a crofter's house upon the road-side, half a mile south-west from

---

[1] Mr. Sands discovered part of the east gable of this chapel—3½ feet thick.—*Proc. Soc. Antiq. Scot.*, vol. xvi. p. 463.

[2] Mr. Sands also mentions (*Ibid.*) that he found some of the mortar and stones of the ancient chapel which evidently here existed; and further, that a stone, with a cross upon it, still forms part of the pavement at Hynish farm-steading. This cross we did not happen to observe, although we stabled at Hynish several times.

the former ferry at the north end of Tiree. The spot where the last interment was made (remembered by an old man only recently dead) was even pointed out in the south-west corner; there are neither signs nor local tradition of a chapel, although Dr. Reeves is doubtless correct in stating that one existed.

Upon this croft was recently found a perforated stone hammer, the hole so perfectly polished, with an outward bevel, as to point to its having undergone a secondary use in the character of a socket for the pivot of a gate.

On the west edge of the road, directly opposite the former burying-ground, are two large stones imbedded in the soil, and between these the Cross of Caoles is said to have stood until taken away to serve in the erection of a house not far off. The tops of these two stones (the socket of the cross) are now nearly level with the adjacent soil, that to the south measuring about 30 by 12 inches upon its exposed end. With this large imbedded stone (perhaps in order to prevent its sharing the fate of the cross itself) is associated a monitory tradition to the effect that, should it ever be removed, a hurricane will follow such as to shake the whole of the island. Upon more than one ground, may the truth of this prophecy never be tested!

The foregoing exhausts Dr. Reeves' list of the ancient chapels in Tiree, but upon the testimony of at least two elderly natives we are able to add the name and dedication of still another +XIV chapel upon the outskirts of Scarinish itself. This is CAIBEAL THOMAIS (the chapel of St. Thomas, pronounced 'Homish') the site of which, with its burying-ground, is immediately to the north-west of the village, about 60 yards south of the Gott road, and 50 yards east of the fence of Scarinish farm. One of our informants told us that his father remembered stones in position there within the last century, and indeed that the chapel ruins were utilised to build the old store on the east side of the harbour.

A field in the glebe, about half a mile north from Scarinish, on the south-west side of the road and manse, is still known as *Tir a' Chaibeil*. This name seems equally to bear the interpretation of 'the land of the chapel,' or 'the chapel lands,' but about its centre are the foundations of the east and west walls of some building, which appears to have measured about 50 by 18 feet, perhaps including an annexe.

Again on the east shoulder of Cnoc Grianal, a rocky green knoll upon Ben Hynish, half a mile east from Balaphuil, is a flat grassy space containing in its centre the foundations of some old building. This has apparently been an oblong oval measuring about 4 by 6 yards over the walls, and from its situation and east and west position may possibly have been another chapel; the comparative isolation of this spot from any of the known ecclesiastical remains, and the frequency of these in other parts of the island, lending all the greater likelihood to the existence of one in this locality also. With a chapel in practically every township—even in small ones so closely adjoining as Kenovay, Cornaig-mor, and Kilmoluag—it is only to be expected that there was one at Balaphuil.

CHAPTER XV

CHARACTERISTICS OF THE DUNS AND SANDHILL-SITES OF COLL AND TIREE

ALTHOUGH involving a certain amount of repetition, it is thought advisable to give here a brief analysis of the various types of Duns in these islands, as also of the few relics which have been found in these and the Sandhill sites, as bearing upon their probable date and ancient occupation.

In the first place, neither island contains any distinctly marked specimen of the Broch or so-called 'Pictish tower' proper,[1] a type of ordinary occurrence in Sutherland, Caithness, Orkney and Shetland, and also represented by a fine group in Glenelg (Inverness-shire), and by a few specimens in the 'Long Island' or outer Hebrides, as well as outlying examples in Perthshire, Stirlingshire, Selkirkshire, and Berwickshire.

To quote, at some length, from Dr. Joseph Anderson's description,[2] 'the typical form of the Broch is that of a hollow circular tower of dry-built masonry about 60 feet in diameter and about 50 feet high. The wall, which is 15 feet thick, is carried up solid for about 8 feet, except where two or three oblong chambers, with rudely

---

[1] Although it is barely possible that some of Class A belong to this type.

[2] *Proc. Soc. Antiq. Scot.*, vol. xii. pp. 314-316.

vaulted roofs, are constructed in its thickness. Above the height of about 8 feet the wall is carried up with a hollow space of about 3 feet wide between its exterior and interior shell. This hollow space, at about the height of a man, is crossed horizontally by a roof of slabs, the upper surfaces of which form the floor of the space above. This is repeated at about every 5 or 6 feet of its further height. These spaces thus form horizontal galleries separated from each other vertically by the slabs of their floors and roofs.' Dr. Anderson states further that the only opening to the outside of the tower is the main entrance, a narrow passage usually about 15 feet long and 3 feet wide, leading straight through the wall on the ground level to the central area or courtyard of the tower, ' round the inner circumference of which, in different positions, are placed the entrances to the chambers on the ground floor, and to the staircase leading to the galleries above. In its external aspect the tower is a truncated cone of solid masonry, unpierced by any opening save the narrow doorway; while the central court presents the aspect of a circular well 30 feet in diameter . . . presenting at intervals on the ground floor several low and narrow doorways giving access to the chambers and stair, and above these ranges of small window-like openings rising perpendicularly over each other to admit light and air to the galleries.'

It is now generally admitted by antiquaries of authority that these Brochs [1] range from a period approximating to that between

[1] According to Skene's *Celtic Scotland*, (second edition, vol. i. pp. 40, 80, 83, 94), the independent tribes of North Britain appear for the first time in A.D. 306 under the general name of 'Picts,' of which one section was known as the *Caledonii*, while in the other are to

the Roman occupation which ended A.D. 410 and the Norse occupation of the Hebrides together with the northern and western parts of Scotland, which commenced before A.D. 800 and continued until 1266. This would give a period for the prevalence of the Brochs of from *ca.* A.D. 300 until *ca.* A.D. 1200.[1] Perhaps a still safer chronology (with regard to the latest excavations) would assign to the Brochs a more general period, viz.—the first eight or ten centuries of the Christian era—thus overlapping, for half that space, with the *whole* duration of the Roman occupation of southern Scotland (A.D. 79-410), a circumstance which need hardly stand in the way, since their special region or habitat was barely infringed upon by the Romans.

be recognised the *Mœatœ* ; the last named consisting of those tribes which were situated next the Antonine Wall (between the Forth and Clyde) on the north, with the *Caledonii* lying yet beyond them. Of these, the *Caledonii* had been separately mentioned in A.D. 65 and the *Mœatœ* A.D. 201, following which data it would appear that the Picts had been established in Scotland about the Christian era, if not, indeed, many years earlier.

The Picts are supposed to have come to Scotland from Wales or Ireland (mythically originating in Thrace or Scythia) and the Scots or Dalriads from the north-east of Ireland. It seems certain that both nations were Celtic in race and language, their dialects bearing probably much the same relation to each other as do the Breton, Welsh, and Cornish (*Ibid.*, vol. i. pp. 194-201 ; also Reeves' *Adamnan*, p. 63).

Skene (*Celtic Scotland*, vol. i. pp. 198-201) indeed states that St. Columba conversed freely with Brude, King of the Northern Picts, and with his messengers, without the intervention of an interpreter ; although upon two occasions he did employ this assistance when expounding the Christian gospel to the Picts, such aid thus appearing to become necessary only when an absolute precision of expression was essential.

It was at the very end of the fourth century, coincident with the final withdrawal of the Romans, that the Picts and Scots formed settled kingdoms in Scotland. The southern Picts were converted to Christianity by St. Ninian, *ca.* 397 ; the northern Picts, under King Brude, in 565 by St. Columba.

[1] Roman coins and fragments of Samian ware have been found in the Brochs of Orkney and Caithness.

These detailed references to the Brochs or 'Pictish Towers' are deemed necessary from the existence in Tiree of the ruins of at least four large Duns which seem certainly (as also four to eight others, less distinctly) to come into a type (Class A) which we have denominated semi-Brochs and described as a connecting link between the Brochs proper and the rude Hill-Forts.

The analogy between the semi-Broch type and the true Brochs consists in their generally massive and circular form with double concentric walls and an intervening passage on the ground floor of 28 to 36 inches wide, although in the true Broch the base is solid except as regards several separate oblong cells and the entrance to the stairway, while the galleries are placed in tiers above the first story. These upper galleries, together with the necessary staircase, appear to be quite absent in our Class A. Indeed it does not seem that the Duns which we have so classed ever reached more than 12 to 15 feet in height, since in no instance could any sign of an upper gallery or a staircase be now observed. It is admitted that this is only negative evidence, but in the other event, it would simply follow that Class A consists of true Brochs, so much ruined that no trace of upper galleries or staircase can now be found, although even then the more or less continuous passage or gallery between the walls on the ground level still differentiates them from the Brochs.

Upon the whole, it seems that Class A is essentially distinct both from the true Brochs or 'Pictish Towers' and from our

Class B—the Rock- or Hill-Forts.   In neither of these two last-named types is present the regular passage of 28 to 36 inches between concentric walls upon the ground floor; and while the semi-Broch agrees with the Broch of Caithness, Orkney, etc., in its symmetrical and massive circular construction, it equally differs in this respect from Class B, where occurs a series of successive ramparts most irregular both in outline and interval. Further, the double main walls of Class A appear to have been distinctly higher than in Class B, and yet not nearly so lofty (with no appearance whatever of staircase or upper galleries) as compared with those of the Broch proper.   We are thus confirmed in the opinion that Class A is quite a separate one,—not impossibly a type which intervened between the rude Rock-Forts and the true Brochs.

It has already been suggested that the groups of small circular cells, of which traces occur within the central keeps of three out of the four semi-Brochs in Class A, may be remains of a secondary occupation, although in Dun Mor Vaul especially, where these are best defined, it would almost appear that they formed part of the original plan.

Class B—of Rock-Forts or Hill-Forts—demands little general description, each Dun being characterised by an irregular individuality of shape and outworks dependent upon the natural configuration of its site.   As a rule, however, there have been at least two or three outer ramparts shielding the point of approach, the other portions being usually protected by steep cliffs or rocks to seaward.

Class C—the Marsh-Duns, upon mounds in present marshes or former lochs—are much larger in size than Class D—Islet Duns—but unfortunately so greatly ruined as to afford little or nothing in the way of ground-plan. The one exception in this respect is Dun Ibrig, where the series of ruined walls suggests the possibility of this type having approached, or even having been identical with, Class A. All of this type have evidently been approached by raised causeways.

Class D—the Islet-Duns—are of comparatively small dimensions, roughly circular in form, but with walls of no great strength, upon islets in most cases at least partly natural. In every instance there seems to have been an access by means of a stone causeway (1 or 2 yards in width and 20 to 30 in length) entirely artificial and not straight but more or less curved. It would appear that much greater importance was placed upon the easily defensible nature of this causeway than upon the walls of the fort itself.

Associated with a few of the Duns already described are special features, to which reference may briefly be made. Within the centre of the otherwise totally ruined Dun Balaphetrish in Tiree, is a built well, with steps leading down; and within the outworks of Dun Mor Vaul is a smaller well; while in at least two other cases similar provision for water-supply is noticeable close at hand. Again, in two Duns—that at Balaphetrish, just mentioned, and Dun Coirbidh, in Coll—there are in each case distinct traces of a narrow pathway up the steep west side, evidently a subsidiary access quite apart from the regular main entrance.

In three or four instances there seem to be cleared, and even guarded, approaches in connection with Duns. This has been noted at Dun Borbaidh in Coll, and is observable with special distinctness at Dun Hiader and Dun na Cleite in Tiree, while slighter indications of a similar pass occur near Dun Beg Vaul.

Two Rock-Forts—Dun Cruit, off Lunga in the Treshnish Isles, and that upon Eilean Dubh (Tiree, No. 16)—appear to have been furnished with rude draw-bridges. Dun Cruit indeed is so precipitous that such a mode of access seems to be the only one possible.

Attention may also be drawn to earthworks or screens at both ends of Loch Cliad (Coll, No. 27), and to another near the Island Dun in Loch Rathilt (Coll, No. 24); and also to the long underground passage traditionally associated with Dunan Nighean (Tiree, No. 13).

As to the date of erection of the various types of Duns in Coll and Tiree, all that can be definitely stated is that they (or at least most of them) are apparently of not later origin than the period of the Norse occupation of the Hebrides, which ceased in A.D. 1266.[1] This is evidenced by the Scandinavian names associated to the present day with several—such as DUN ANLAIMH in Coll (in Loch nan Cinneachan, 'the loch of the heathen,' tradition also connecting an *Olaf* with DUN ACHA); DUN HIADER, DUN IBRIG, and DUN OTTIR, all in Tiree; apart from the generic Norse *borg* represented in BORBAIDH and

---

[1] While, on the other hand, they may date back to about (or before) the Christian era.

BORAIGE, also the significant DUN NAN GALL, and DUN CRUIT (*Cruithne* = 'a Pict') upon a precipitous rock off Lunga in the Treshnish Isles.[1]

The word *Borg* enters not uncommonly into place-names in Iceland, and it is recorded (as noted in the next chapter) that Bjorn the Easterling, son of Ketil Flatnef, had his residence from *ca.* A.D. 886 at *Borgarholt*, and was buried near the neighbouring streamlet *Borgarlækr*, in the valley of Vididal (or *Willow-dale*). *Borg* certainly has had the further meaning of *town* or *village*, but the derivative seems clearly to represent a *fortification* or *defence*, which in those days was ordinarily the nucleus of a village.[2] We find Bardi, of the 'Heath-Slayings,'[3] associated *ca.* A.D. 1013-1021, with Litla-Borg and Stora-Borg in Iceland, where, between these two homesteads, upon the basaltic cone of Borgarvirki (at a height of some 800 feet above the sea-level) are still the ruins of a fine stone-fort, resembling in its massive exterior the best preserved of the semi-Brochs of Tiree, although it appears to have been a Rock-Fort pure and simple, without any passage or ground gallery within the outer wall.[4]

[1] From this list are purposely omitted any which seem to be merely place-names of Norse derivation; as Gott, Sgibinis, Heanish, Hanais, Vaul, and Salum; with Foulag and Beic, possibly also of non-Gaelic origin. In the Outer Hebrides a similar nomenclature is equally suggestive.

[2] Cleasby and Vigfusson's *An Icelandic-English Dictionary*, p. 73.

[3] *The Saga Library*, vol. ii. pp. xliii, 366.

[4] Borgarvirki is figured and described in Collingwood and Stefansson's *A Pilgrimage to the Saga-Steads of Iceland*, pp. 154-157, Ulverston, 1899, and seems to be a practical contribution to the debated question of the erection of stone-forts in Scotland by the Norsemen. It is also minutely described by Dr. Bjorn M. Olsen of Reykjavik in *Arbok hins*

In Norway itself there exist a number of stone forts (known as *Bygdeborge*) somewhat similar to Borgarvirki and certainly ancient, although it does not appear that any definite period is assigned to them.[1]

But indeed it seems in every way most probable that the Hebridean Duns were the work of a native[2] race, and had been (in general, at least) erected prior to the more or less continuous domination by the Norsemen, who may have taken possession of these forts and occupied them, but would scarcely have permitted such strongholds to be constructed by the race or races whom they held under their yoke.[3]

The conjecture logically follows that most of the Duns in these islands had been built either *before* or *at* a period coincident with the first forays of the Vikings,[4] of date about A.D. 800,

islenzka fornleifafjelags, 1880-1881 (Year-book of the Icelandic Antiquarian Society), pp. 99-113 ; and in Daniel Bruun's *Arkæologiske undersogelser paa Island*, Copenhagen, 1899.

[1] Described by O. Rygh, 'Gamle Bygdeborge i Norge,' in *Foreningen til norske fortidsmindesmerkers bevaring, Aarsberetning for* 1882, pp. 30–80.

[2] Although some of the Hebridean Forts may perhaps have been built by the Norsemen. As to period, such an hypothesis would merely extend the possible origin of these Duns until the first half of the thirteenth century. It must be acknowledged, in making this *caveat*, that no relic of distinctly Norse type is recorded from any Broch or Dun in Scotland. Upon the other hand, the few objects discovered are of most indefinite class, consisting chiefly of rough hammer-stones or 'pounders' and crude pottery.

[3] In the Icelandic Sagas are recorded two temporary Norse occupations of the Broch of Mousa (Moseyjar-borg) in Shetland at an interval of some 250 years. The first in date was *ca.* A.D. 900, and the second *ca.* A.D. 1155 (Anderson's *Orkneyinga Saga*, pp. cxi and 161 ; also *Scotland in Pagan Times, The Iron Age*, pp. 200-201).

[4] The Irish 'Scots' are said to have first invaded Scotland about A.D. 360, the Picts then forming the inhabitants of Britain north of the Forth and Clyde (Skene's *Celtic Scotland*, second edn., vol. iii. p. 125) ; while it is generally agreed that the Dalriads (also Irish Scots,

while the intervening duration of the Norse supremacy (say *ca.* 900-1000 until their final withdrawal in 1266) would exclude any later date for their origin.

This indeed seems thoroughly compatible with the mention, by ancient annalists, of Forts in various districts of Scotland.[1] Moreover, in times approaching the historic period, we find specific dates attached in the Irish chronicles to notices of several Duns.

'the Sons of Erc') permanently settled in the (now) county of Argyllshire about A.D. 506 (Reeves' *Adamnan*, p. 433). This denotes a still earlier invasion against which the Picts would naturally fortify themselves, especially on the western shore, where indeed we find most of the Duns.

[1] A still earlier (although perhaps entirely legendary) people, named the *Firbolg*—a small dark race—is said to have preceded the Picts in Ireland. Expelled from Ireland by another tribe, the *Tuatha De Danaan*, they occupied part of the Hebrides, until driven out thence by the Cruithnigh or Picts. This account may be largely mythical, but it is at least interesting to note that the site of an ancient fort in St. Kilda is known as *Dun-Fhirbolg* (Skene's *Celtic Scotland*, vol. i. pp. 173-185). The *Annals of the Four Masters* place the arrival of the Milesians or Scots in Ireland as *anno mundi* 3500, or B.C. 1694 (*Ibid.*, vol. i. p. 180), but, without urging this remote antiquity, there can be little question that the Scots were in *Ireland* long before the Roman invasion of Britain.

In the Aran Isles (off the Galway coast) are two very large and elaborate forts—Dun Aengus and Dun Conor—to which tradition assigns a date of the first century A.D. Dun-Fhirbolg, in St. Kilda, has just been mentioned, and—again to follow legend, our only authority—several sites of Duns or Forts in the West of Scotland which are referred to a period not far distant from the Christian era, can still be identified. Of these, one is *Dunskaith* (at Sleat in Skye), said to be named after *Scathaidh* who there conducted a military school and educated the five grandsons of Cathbad, 'a Druid of the Picts of Ulster,' viz., Cuchullin, the three sons of Uisneach, and Conall Cearnach. Associated with the last-named is *Dunchonill* upon one of the Garveloch Isles, and with the sons of Uisneach—'the Three Dragons of Dunmonadh,'—are particularly *Dun mhic Uisneachan* (the *Beregonium* of Boece) on the north side of Loch Etive, and, more incidentally, *Dunadd* and *Duntroon*, at Crinan, and *Dun Suibhne* (or Castle Swen) in Knapdale (*Ibid.*, vol. iii. pp. 127-130). These are of course from Fingalian legends.

The earliest of these

'Bellum Duin-bolg,' *anno* 598, and

'Bellum Duin-Ceithirn,' *anno* 629 (also 681),

apparently both refer to Irish sites, but the following

'Bellum Duin-locho,' 678 ;

'Obsessio Duin-Baitte,' 680 ;

'Obsessio Duin-Foither,' 681 (and again, 694) ;

'Obsessio Duin-Att, et Duin-Duirn,' 683 ;

'Bellum Duin-Nechtain,' 686 ;

'Combustio Tula-aman Duin-Ollaigh,' 686, as also

'Combustio Duin Onlaigh, 698 ;

'Destructio Duin Onlaigh apud Selbach,' 701 ;

'Dun-Ollaigh construitur apud Selbacum,' 714 ;

'Obessio Dun-Deauæ,' 692 ;

'Obsessio Aberte apud Selbachum,' 712 ;

seem in every case to be identified with Scottish (and several of them with West-Scottish) localities.[1]

Having regard to the historical facts—and legendary traditions

---

[1] Reeves' *Adamnan*, pp. 372-381. *Dun-locho* is coupled with *Doirad Eilind*—'obviously the island of Jura.' *Dun Baitte* is supposed to represent Dun-beath in Caithness, and *Dun-Foither*, Dunotter near Stonehaven, or Forteviot in Perthshire ; *Dun-Att* and *Dun-Duirn* are evidently Dun-add near the Crinan Canal, and Dundurn in Perthshire ; *Dun-Nechtan* seems to be Dunnichen in Forfarshire ; while *Dun-Ollaigh* is almost certainly Dunolly near Oban, the chief stronghold of the *Cinel Loarn* or race of Lorne, with whom St. Columba was closely allied by birth, being the grandson of Erca, daughter of Loarn Mor, (Selbach being tenth in descent from the last named). *Aberte* is supposed to be Dunaverty in Kintyre, and 'Tula Aman' to represent Tulli-Almond in Perthshire. These details and identifications are entirely cited from Skene's *Celtic Scotland* and Reeves' *Adamnan*, where the quotations are nearly all from the *Annals of Ulster*, with two or three from Tighernach.

(no more are available)—already adduced, it seems reasonable to judge that for the first eight hundred years of our era the Hebrides were mainly possessed by the Picts, a race subjected, especially as time progressed, to incursions from a distinctly kindred people, the Irish Scots, who indeed gave to Ireland the name *Scotia* which only secondarily devolved upon Scotland— formerly known as *Caledonia* or part of *Britannia*.

The next definite epoch of Hebridean history lies between the first Viking raids, commencing (so far as we know) about A.D. 800, and the final surrender of the Norwegian suzerainty in 1266—a subject treated at greater length in our next chapter.

We have already shown that Duns or Forts are recorded as existing in Scotland (and the Hebrides) from *at latest* the seventh century A.D., with one knows not what margin of earlier origin.

Our deduction would be that the Hebridean Duns—taking them in the most general way—may be regarded as belonging to a period ranging from somewhere about the Christian era to the years 900—1000 A.D. The terminal epoch (as already suggested) is derived from the undoubted supremacy which the Norsemen attained in the Hebrides or Sudreys, and the more likely occasion for the erection of these Forts would appear to have been the incursions from Ireland *before* the coming of the Vikings, unless indeed they were built during the transition stage, when the visits of the Norsemen were less frequent, and their authority was not yet fully established. In either case we give them a date of not later than about A.D. 1000, with quite a thousand years of possible earlier chronology.

Dismissing this subject, and coming to more congenial facts, most of the Duns in Coll and Tiree are close to the western shores of these islands. A not unreasonable inference is that the occupants expected their foes from seaward—whether from Ireland or Norway.[1] Further, the Duns—more especially upon the west shores—as a rule stand in a continuous chain, each within view of the next; so notably indeed that in several instances a fresh site has been discovered by searching a headland between two forts already known, but obstructed by it from an interchange of signals. If any such communication really existed, it was possibly by means of fire—showing smoke by day, or flame by night. This method is the traditionary one, while it also appeals to the sense of the probable. Several Duns in both Coll and Tiree are not indeed within full view of each other, and yet in each of these cases, smoke or flames might well have served as a warning from one to the other.

Apart from the names of Norse derivation which are still attached to several of the Duns, the argument (to which we freely defer) is that, whatever their after occupation, they were of native, *i.e.* Pictish or Celtic, origin.[2] Two of the forts which we notice lend special testimony to this, the approved, view. These are, first, the Dun (or Duns) in Loch Cliad in Coll, where, at each end of the Loch, is a distinct long and straight earth-

---

[1] It is true that the same holds good with the west coast of Ireland, where enemies could scarcely be expected from the Atlantic.

[2] The Norsemen of the Viking time are said never to have erected *stone* forts at home. There, indeed, they had abundance of wood; but see pp. 165-166 for Borgarvirki in Iceland, and the Norwegian *Bygdeborge*.

work—sloped outside, but abrupt within—clearly as if a mask from outer observation. The other instance is in connection with Dunan Nighean in Tiree, where there is said to have been a narrow underground passage from close to the Dun's entrance, first through a natural lateral fault in the rock, then under a sandbank of considerable present size, and emerging on the shore—at a distance of some 200 yards from its commencement—through another, or the same, cleft in the strata.

Dun Cruit—on Lunga, one of the Treshnish Isles—is by its name associated with the Picts. It is incidentally curious to note that the subjugation of the Picts by Kenneth MacAlpin in 844 so nearly coincides with the first recorded permanent occupation of the Sudreys by the Norsemen, under Ketil Flatnef, before the year 852.

If we take the Duns in Coll and Tiree at about thirty in each island, and allow an average of three families to those in Coll and four in Tiree (having regard to their relative size), a theoretic Dun-population of some 450 for Coll and 600 for Tiree is easily deduced, upon the assumption that these forts were simultaneously occupied. This seems to be no excessive estimate, and would give to Coll, for its Duns alone, a census quite equalling that of the whole island at the present day, and similarly in Tiree would account for about one-third of its actual population, which is comparatively much denser than in Coll. This calculation is altogether apart from the separate occupants both of the Sandhills and of the remoter inland parts of the islands, who might well aggregate to an equal number, although it is by no means certain that the Sandhill dwellers were of coeval date with those of the forts.

In the present chapter it has already been suggested that some, at least, of the Duns of Coll and Tiree were annexed and occupied by the Norwegian intruders—this being almost proved by the Norse names which several still bear, in addition to local legends concerning two in Coll, Dun Acha and Dun Anlaimh. Again, it seems in every way probable, that men of the 'broken' clans—who are recorded upon authority as existing in Coll in 1587 [1]—would select the remoter forts as most convenient dwellings to afford shelter and a certain amount of defensive security. These 'broken men' appear to have been simply companies of freebooters, entirely beyond the reach of the then legal authority, who adopted the Viking principle of living at the expense of those who were weaker than themselves. Indeed, there can be no question that some of the Duns were inhabited well within historic times. [2]

[1] See Chapter VII. page 59.

[2] *Scotland in Pagan Times, The Iron Age*, pp. 270-271. The latest distinct reference to the occupation of these minor Island Forts seems to be contained in the *Reg. Privy Council*, where (vol. viii. p. 522) it is recorded that King James VI. set himself in earnest (*anno* 1608) to the complete subjugation of the Highlands and Islands. By virtue of a royal commission, a small fleet was despatched from Ayr in the summer of that year, under Lord Ochiltree and Andrew, Bishop of the Isles, to reduce to obedience the clans in the Hebrides from Islay to Mull ; Coll and Tiree being specially mentioned in the reports. From an official letter from Lord Ochiltree, 12th August 1608, this expedition consisted of 'two Inglishe shippis, the one under the conduct of Sir Williame Sanct Johnne, callit "The Advantage," quha behavis himselff verie cairfullie and honestlie in all occasionis of this service, the other under the government of Owne Wenne, ane followar of the other with ane pynnage with other tua Scottis shippis of my awne, togidder with ten barkis' ; the whole company being 'in nomber scairse nyne hundreth men,' who (according to a previous minute, *Ibid.*, p. 60) were 'weil

But the whole subject of these ancient forts is in every way a most difficult one, and when we come to analyse the relics of their past inhabitants, as disclosed through a perfunctory excavation of their kitchen-middens, nothing can be found to identify them with any definite race or era; although upon other grounds, as above explained, we are satisfied that they were constructed by the native inhabitants, and may have been occasionally occupied by the Norsemen.

A list of objects found in the Duns of Coll and Tiree is here annexed, precedence being given according to the comparative frequency of occurrence.

1. Kitchen-midden ashes, bones (one deer-horn), and shells.

> The bones are usually split (evidently to extract the marrow) and sometimes bear transverse cuts. Horses' teeth are fairly common in some of the Duns, but so far as could be observed, by no means of invariable occurrence.

providit and furneist with munitioun, poulder and bullet.' Lord Ochiltree's commission was to destroy 'lumfaddis, birlingis and heyland gallayis' (so far as not required for peaceful uses, and really referring to war boats), and to demolish 'the houssis and strenthis pertening to the saidis rebellious, unansuerable and dissobedient personis' (*Ibid.*, p. 741; 'the castellis and houssis of strength' occurring on p. 739). This expedition proved most successful ; indeed, by a stratagem—which included the temptations of a sermon by the Bishop of the Isles, and a dinner to follow, on board the king's ship 'The Moon' (*Ibid.*, p. lviii)—the most dangerous of the chiefs were taken prisoners ; and following thereupon an important agreement, 'The Band and Statutes of Icolmkill,' was executed 23 Aug. 1609, breaking up the independent clan rule, and giving (at least nominally) a full submission to the central government.

It must be added, however, that *The Acts of the Parliament of Scotland* (Thomson, vol. vi. part 2., p. 168, *anno* 1649) describe the inhabitants of 'Mull, Teirie, Coill,' etc., as having been practically all 'in actuall rebellioun' about the years 1645-1647; and indeed throughout the seventeenth century, in various parts of the Highlands, many of the clansmen were content to remain outlaws.

Fish-bones and, more especially, the shells of the limpet and periwinkle, were usually found, with occasional oyster-shells and crab-claws; but shell-fish do not seem to have formed so predominant an article of diet in the Duns as in the Sandhill dwellings.

2. Hammer-stones — water-worn stones of oval or oblong-oval shape, and greatly varying in size, just as gathered from the beach, but with distinct marks of use on one or both ends, sometimes to an extreme extent, and occasionally upon both edges also. Less frequently these stones, when of flattish form, bear indentations in the centre of their sides, as if caused by their use as hammers upon metal chisels. Otherwise the hammer-stones seem chiefly to have been employed in pounding. Sometimes a large group was found—with or without the marks of use—which bore signs of fire, having evidently been raised to a high temperature. In this connection the reasonable explanation is offered that they had been used for heating water in large earthenware vessels by being inserted therein. Only a single hammer-stone (see Plate facing p. 8) can be noted as bearing at all the appearance of a weapon; this is symmetrically shaped and bevelled off at the base on both sides. All the others seem to have been purely domestic implements.

3. Fragments of a coarse pottery (always unglazed) are very common, though no complete vessel was found, and

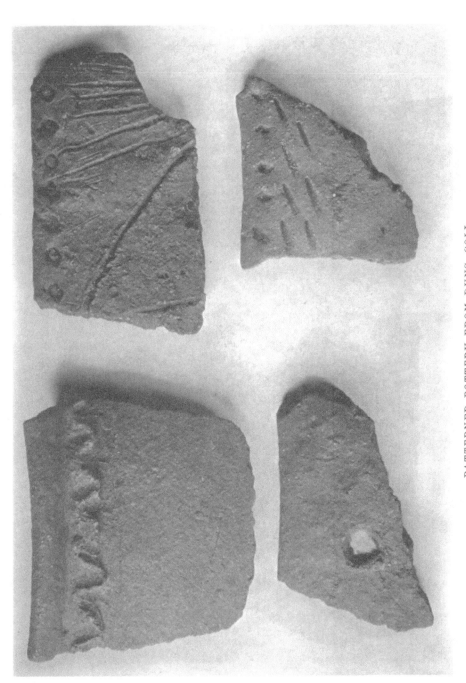

PATTERNED POTTERY FROM DUNS—COLL,

No. 1, ACTUAL SIZE.

PATTERNED POTTERY FROM DUNS—COLL,

No. 2, ACTUAL SIZE.

PATTERNED POTTERY FROM DUNS—COLL,

No. 3, ACTUAL SIZE.

PATTERNED POTTERY FROM DUNS—COLL.

No. 4, ACTUAL SIZE.

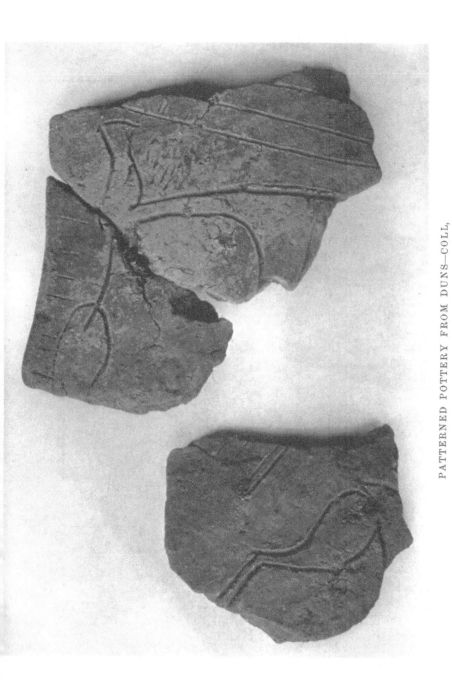

PATTERNED POTTERY FROM DUNS—COLL,

No. 5, ACTUAL SIZE.

(*Note.*—The smaller fragment is inverted.)

PATTERNED POTTERY FROM DUNS—TIBEE,

No. 6, ACTUAL SIZE.

PATTERNED POTTERY—TIREE,

No. 7, ACTUAL SIZE.

PATTERNED POTTERY FROM DUNS—TIREE,

No. 8, ACTUAL SIZE.

PATTERNED POTTERY FROM DUNS—TIREE,

No. 9, ACTUAL SIZE.

PATTERNED POTTERY FROM DUNS—TIREE,

No. 10, ACTUAL SIZE.

only one of undoubted Dun origin was met with. In some cases, however, the pieces were sufficiently large to show the size and shape of the vessel, evidently in two instances resembling the bowl of a small wine-glass, and in a third, a shallow saucer. Most of the pottery was entirely plain—apart from a very simple rim—but a great variety of patterns was also found, ranging from the crudest row of ridges, formed by the human finger-nail, to zig-zag ornament and even occasional attempts to imitate the fern leaf, with (quite exceptionally, at Dun Borbaidh in Coll) the figure of a stag. The commonest patterns are in short lines, simple or crossed, incised by some small sharp tool, such as a flint, a pointed bone, or metal pin. These patterns are all *indented*, but there is another rarer class with *raised* ornament (always near the rim) usually in the form of a zig-zag or wave. One fragment of a plain pot was found with a well-shaped perforation nearly an inch below the lip of the vessel, evidently to admit a rude cord or handle by which it could be carried or suspended.

4 Small water-worn pebbles (very plentiful in many of the Duns) averaging about half an inch to one inch in diameter or length. As to the use of these we can only suggest that they may have been sling-stones.

5. Flint is rare in the Duns (quite contrary to the case of the Sandhill dwellings) and always in the form of small nodules or flaked pieces, never sufficiently shaped

to deserve the name of scrapers. Indeed they seem rather to bear the character of strike-lights. Flints were observed at only about one-fifth of the whole of the Duns noted.

6. One slate-whorl and one pottery-whorl were unearthed. We know definitely of three more of the latter having been discovered, and have had reports of several others.

7. Small pieces of shaped bone, either rounded like a pin, or squared and then brought to a point. But these are very scarce. Also a single bone holed through its thicker end.

8. A very few fragments of much corroded metal (chiefly, if not entirely, iron) of too indeterminate form to decide their purposes, yet clearly shaped to serve some special object. Further, but very rarely, nodules of iron ore, each of something like an ounce in weight.

Comparing the above *résumé* of the Dun relics with the corresponding results from the Sandhills, we there find—

1. Kitchen-midden ashes, bones, and shells—the latter in great abundance.

2. Hammer-stones, of medium to very large size, are quite as common as in the Duns.

3. Pottery is very plentiful; much of it of a somewhat coarser make, containing more grit and small stones than that of the Duns. Patterned fragments are quite scarce, and the few varieties of design are mainly of a slight and

HAMMER-STONE FROM TIREE SANDHILLS,

No. 1, ACTUAL SIZE.

HAMMER-STONE FROM TIREE SANDHILLS,

No. 2, ACTUAL SIZE.

HAMMER-STONES FROM TIREE SANDHILLS,

Nos. 3 AND 4, ACTUAL SIZE.

PATTERNED POTTERY FROM SANDHILLS—COLL,

No. 1, ACTUAL SIZE.

PATTERNED POTTERY FROM SANDHILLS—TIREE,

No. 2, ACTUAL SIZE.

simple nature—mere rows of very small indentations or lines, or small rings as if produced by the hollow stem of a rush.

5. Flints are abundant, occurring at every one of the Sand-hill sites, and frequently including scrapers. Flint-knives are uncommon, and only two arrow-heads were noticed.

7. One holed-bone was found.

8. Lumps of iron slag are not rare, as also fragments of wrought rivets, etc. The same importance cannot, how-ever, be attached to these as to metal from the Duns, since they may be relics of the Viking period super-imposed upon the earlier occupation of the Sandhills.

9. Several bone and bronze pins. One needle and a large bodkin, both well-shaped from bone, and found near each other.

Patterned pottery was noted at only four Duns in Coll, but at eleven in Tiree. To some extent it was found to occur upon almost all the Sandhill sites in both islands.

A small proportion of the pottery may represent fragments of sepulchral urns, of which none are known to exist in connection with so late a period as the Iron Age deposits in Scotland.[1]

---

[1] *Scotland in Pagan Times, Bronze and Stone Ages*, p. 3.

CHAPTER XVI

THE NORWEGIAN OCCUPATION OF THE HEBRIDES

PROFESSOR P. A. MUNCH in his most valuable treatise upon *The Chronicle of Man and the Sudreys* assigns to the Scottish Hebrides (*Sudreyjar*, or 'southern isles') an important place in the earlier pages of Norwegian history, as having formed 'for about 170 years at least' (*i.e.* A.D. 1098-1266), 'if not for double that time' (*ca.* 880-1266), a part of the Norse kingdom. It must indeed be admitted that, as to the earlier half of the last-mentioned period, this occupation was chiefly an unsettled one, somewhat casual and irregular in its nature, and attributable rather to the Norse pirates or vikings than to any systematic control by the kings of Norway.

The ancient Sagas[1] (or histories) of Norway, Iceland, and Orkney contain many brief references to our Hebrides, but these are usually so incidental and fragmentary that little of any definite nature is to be gleaned either concerning specific localities, or as to details of the invasions or the general occupation of these islands. It has been the writer's endeavour to include

---

[1] These chronicles, indeed, until about the time of King Harald Harfagri (*ca.* 853), seem to be mere legends, and to contain almost as much myth as history.

in the present chapter a *résumé* of all the more striking references to be identified with our local subject from those of the Sagas which are readily available.

From as early as about the year 789, the Norsemen, in their 'vestrviking,'[1] or western piracy, had been accustomed to harry (with some regularity) the coasts of England, Scotland, and Ireland. Dr. Joseph Anderson in his Introduction to *The Orkneyinga Saga* quotes the *Anglo-Saxon Chronicle*, under date 787, as to King Beorhtric, that 'in his days first came three ships of Northmen from Hæretha-land' (Horda-land on the west coast of Norway), and that these were the first 'Danish' (or more correctly, *Norse*) rovers who sought England.[2] In 793 or 795 the Norsemen attacked the Irish shores, in 798 they plundered the Hebrides, and again in 802 and 806 are recorded to have visited and ravaged Iona.[3] These raids were, however,

[1] 'Viking' does not ordinarily bear the meaning of 'sea-king,' but rather that of a 'bay-rover,' although in some cases vikings happened also to be sea-kings. The derivation is from *vik*, a bay or creek, and *-ing*, a common terminal denoting occupation.

So late as about the year 1170, Swein Asleifson (of Gairsay in Orkney) was a famous viking, accustomed, each season when the seed had been sown, to make a pirate-voyage about the Sudreys and Ireland, returning to Orkney after midsummer from this 'spring-viking.' After harvest he used to make another voyage, called the 'autumn-viking,' reaching home again at the beginning of winter (*Orkneyinga Saga, Rolls* edition, vol. i. p. 218).

[2] Keary, in *The Vikings in Western Christendom*, p. 126, gives this date as 789, and the locality as 'a harbour of the Dorset coast,' inclining also to the belief that these first raiders were Danes, perhaps from Hardeland in Jutland. The famous attack upon Lindisfarne came four years later (*Ibid.*, p. 127), and there seems little reason to doubt that this was by Norsemen, even if the previous descent upon Wessex had been made by their Danish neighbours. It is to be noted that in mediæval history the terms 'Northmen' or 'Danes' often stand for Scandinavians *generally*, and not necessarily in either case for men from Norway or Denmark.

[3] Anderson's *Orkneyinga Saga*, p. xxi ; also Munch, p. ix.

a mere prelude to their further incursions. In 807 they lodged themselves in the north of Ireland, and in 852 Olaf the White[1] took Dublin, and firmly established himself as king in that district. Although there are traces, about this period, of a Norwegian emigration to the Sudreys, it was not until after the battle of Hafursfjord, *ca.* 883, when King Harald Harfagri (*the fair-haired*) consolidated all Norway into one monarchy by subduing the petty kings or jarls, and also invaded the rights of the odallers or freeholders by taking their lands, that the general immigration commenced which resulted in the more thorough Norse occupation of the Hebrides, together with Orkney, Shetland, the Faroes, and even Iceland. Large numbers of the discontented chiefs and their followers fled the country, and Professor Munch specially notes that of the four hundred principal settlers, who first divided Iceland between them (*ca.* 880-900), the greatest and most powerful did not emigrate thither direct from Norway, but from the Sudreys.[2] While this statement is most interesting, and certainly to some large extent correct as concerns the Hebrides (and especially in regard to the children of Ketil Flatnef as is afterwards noted), it can hardly be doubted that the Orkneys and Shetlands would all along be a chief base of operations for the outlawed subjects of Norway, whose connection with these northern islands was of a more complete and permanent nature than their comparatively partial occupation and control of the Sudreys.

[1] In Gaelic 'Amhlabh,' or 'Anlaimh'; descended from the same family as King Harald Harfagri (*Orkneyinga Saga*, p. xxi). His father was 'King' Ingialld, son of Helgi (Dasent's *Burnt Njal*, vol. i. p. 1; and Johnstone's *Antiquitates Celto-Scandicæ*, p. 18).

[2] Munch, p. iii.

Nevertheless, whilst making this fair and moderate concession that the Hebrides 'did not at any period contain large and lasting colonies,' but rather an uncertain and fluctuating population of Norsemen, and that the native Celtic element ' was never entirely absorbed by the Norwegian settlers as in Orkney,' yet it is not to be denied that 'real and lasting settlements were made in many parts of the western islands and that the predominant influence was on the side of the Norwegians,' while the Gaelic population remained always the larger element and their language was chiefly spoken.[1] The above seems to be a most reasonable view of the matter, and merely infers that the comparatively small inducements for permanent settlement (on account of the trifling proportion of arable soil and the general absence of timber, in historic times at least) prevented the planting of any large colonies, and, at the same time, the assimilation of the natives. Generally speaking, it may be safe to assume that the Hebrides were held by a few leading Norsemen and their followers, sufficient to ensure the maintenance of the foreign yoke and to collect tribute.

The first prominent Norwegian settler, whose name appears in the Hebrides, is Ketil Flatnef[2] (Flat-nose), in many ways a very

[1] Munch, pp. v and xviii. Dasent says, of the Sudreys (*Burnt Njal*, vol. i. p. clxxxiv), 'To this day the name of almost every island on the west coast of Scotland is either pure Norse or Norse distorted,' and that, 'while the original inhabitants were not expelled but held in bondage as thralls, the Norsemen must have dwelt, and dwelt thickly upon them too, as conquerors and lords.'

[2] Skene in his *Celtic Scotland*, second edition, vol. i. p. 312, identifies Ketil Flatnef with Caittil Finn of the *Annals of Ulster*. *The Saga of King Olaf Tryggwason* (London, 1895), p. 164, makes the sweeping assertion that from Bjorn (Ketil's father) 'were descended almost all the great men of Iceland.'

interesting personage. He had been a man of importance at
home, as the son of Bjorn Buna, a lord of Sogn in Western
Norway, not far from Bergen. By all accounts he must have
established himself in the Sudreys for a considerable time before
the first expedition thither of King Harald Harfagri, which,
although chronicled by Munch as in or about 870, would seem
more naturally to be placed some years later—that is to say, *after*
Harald had become (by his victory of Hafursfjord, *ca.* 883[1])
master of all Norway. According to one statement, Ketil Flatnef
was sent by King Harald to the Hebrides to chastise some
Vikings who had there taken up their abode;[2] but a more
probable version of the story runs to the effect that Ketil
emigrated from Norway to the Sudreys because of his obnoxious-
ness to the king.[3] Be this as it may, Ketil had married one of
his daughters, Aud 'Djupaudga' (the deeply-wealthy) to King
Olaf the White at about the period of the latter's victory at
Dublin (A.D. 852).[4] In connection with the marriage of another

---

[1] King Harald Harfagri was born about 853, and died *ca.* 933-936. Skene (who gives
the former date absolutely) places the battle of Hafursfjord in the year 883 (*Celtic Scotland*,
vol. i. p. 336). This battle is usually assigned to A.D. 872, but Skene's chronology appears
to have reason.

[2] Munch, p. 33, from the *Landnamabok*.

[3] *Ibid.*, from the *Laxdælasaga*.

[4] So says Munch, p. xi, and his statement seems to be approximately correct. Keary,
pp. 293 and 440, mentions that Olaf the White ruled the coast settlements in Ireland, over
Norsemen and Danes alike (Finn-Gaill and Dubh-Gaill), and that the Irish kings themselves
paid him tribute. The same authority records, p. 165, that in the Irish Chronicles, the
Vikings are variously described as 'Sea-robbers,' 'Gentiles' (heathen), 'Gaill' (foreigners),
or 'Lochlann' (lake-men). This latter designation also occurs in the Hebrides.

King Olaf the White and Aud 'the very wealthy' had one son, Thorstein the Red, with
whom, upon his father's death, *ca.* 872 (Munch, p. x), Aud sailed to her relatives in the

daughter, Thorunna Hyrna (the horned)—to Helgi Magri (the Lean), son of Eyvind Eastman,[1]—Ketil Flatnef is described in the *Landnamabok* as 'or Sudreyum' (of the Sudreys),[2] and in the same association his father is named as Bjorn the rough-footed, son of Grim, lord of Sogn.[3] Ketil's wife was Ingvilld, and besides the two daughters above noted (and another named Jorunn) they had two sons, Bjorn the Eastman and Helgi Bjola, both of whom ultimately settled in Iceland, in

Sudreys, where Thorstein married Thurida, daughter of Eyvind Eastman (*Celto-Scand.*, p. 19), aunt and nephew thus wedding brother and sister. Thorstein the Red became a 'herkong' (warrior), and *ca.* 874-880 an ally of Sigurd Riki (the rich), first earl of Orkney, whom he assisted to subdue Caithness, Sutherland, Ross and Moray. After Earl Sigurd's death (*ca.* 880, *Rolls*, vol. i. p. 5) Thorstein ruled these conquered districts until he was himself slain in Caithness (*ca.* 888, *Burnt Njal*, vol. i. p. cci). Upon her son's death Aud went first to Orkney, where she gave her granddaughter Groa (apparently *eldest* daughter of Thorstein the Red and Thurida) in marriage to Duncan, Earl of Caithness (*Celto-Scand.*, p. 19, and *Orkneyinga Saga*, p. xxiii). Since this appears to have happened very soon after Thorstein's fall, and as he is known to have left at least seven children, one of them of about marriageable age at the time of his death, the date of that event cannot have been much, if at all, earlier than the year 888 as given by Dasent in *Burnt Njal* (*supra*). Munch fixes the date as *ca.* 874, but this seems to be quite untenable. Afterwards Aud visited the Faroes, and thence sailed for Iceland, to join her brother Helgi Bjola already settled there at Kialarness. Aud took for herself all the Dale country about Hvamm on Breidafjord; this was about the year 892, and she died in West Iceland 908-910 (*Saga Library*, vol. ii. p. xlix; also *Burnt Njal*, vol. i. pp. lxxx, cci).

Skene states (*Celtic Scotland*, vol. i. pp. 312, 313) that Olaf the White, Norwegian king of Dublin, had (also) married a daughter of King Kenneth I. of Scotland. If this was so, Aud must have been his *second* wife.

[1] Eyvind Eastman (so-called because he was from Götaland in Sweden), son of Bjorn, had married Raforta daughter of Kiarval (or Carrol) King of Dublin or of Ossory, 872-887 (Munch, p. xii; *Orkneyinga Saga*, p. 209; and *Celto-Scand.*, pp. 23, 24).

[2] *Celto-Scand.*, p. 24.

[3] *Burnt Njal*, vol. ii. p. 115. Helgi the Lean went to Iceland (*ca.* 880) and took to himself the whole of Eyjafjord on the north coast; he was a *semi*-Christian (Munch, p. xiv; *Saga Library*, vol. i. pp. xx, xliv, xlv).

each case first visiting the Sudreys, where in 884 Bjorn Eastman found Helgi Bjola and Aud (his father being then dead), and remained with them for two 'winters,'—but disgusted by the fact that his relatives had accepted Christianity he took ship in 886 for Iceland.[1]

Ketil Flatnef had two brothers, Hrapp and Helgi.[2] The first named had a son Orlyg, who was educated by Bishop Patrick in the Sudreys.   Orlyg also sailed for Iceland, provided by the bishop with timber, some consecrated earth, and an iron bell, with instructions to build a church dedicated to St. Columba at a place fully described. All this was duly carried out at Esjuberg upon lands given to Orlyg by his cousin Helgi Bjola (son of Ketil Flatnef) who owned a large district in the west of Iceland.[3] Nothing is known of Ketil's latter years, except that he died in the Sudreys before 884, while it is stated that all of his children, such as were there resident with him, had adopted Christianity.[4] His daughter Aud seems certainly to have become a Christian, as we read of the erection of a cross by her at 'the place of her devotions, a bold and precipitous rock, in the front of the mountain,' this

[1] *Celto-Scand.*, p. 18 ; *Saga Library*, vol. ii. p. 10.   Bjorn had remained in Norway after his father's emigration, but was afterwards outlawed by King Harald Harfagri either because of the non-payment of 'scatt,' or more probably on account of the complete defection of Ketil Flatnef (*Saga Library*, vol. ii. pp. x, xvi, 3-5).   This was in or about 884, ten years after the first settlement of Iceland by Ingolf son of Orn (*Ibid.*, vol. i. p. 192 ; vol. ii. pp. xlix, 6). Bjorn is suggested to have been the only one of Ketil's children who did not renounce paganism ; he settled *ca.* 886 at Burgholt or Borgarholt in Bjarnarhöfn (West Iceland) and was buried there beside the streamlet of Borgarlækr (*Ibid.*, vol. ii. pp. 10, 11, 366, 367).
[2] Munch, pp. xi, xii, and xv.   [3] *Ibid.*, pp. xiv, xv ; *Celto-Scand.*, pp. 14-16.
[4] *Saga Library*, vol. ii. p. 10.

rock being still known, early in the present century, as Kross-holum.[1] Through Aud and her brothers Bjorn and Helgi Bjola, Ketil was the ancestor of many powerful Icelanders.

It may be taken as a fact that there was a Norse emigration of vikings to the Sudreys, continuing for many years before the battle of Hafursfjord, and that these harried not only the western isles, but also their parent country in the summer time. It was this latter fact which provoked King Harald Harfagri's first expedition, ca. 884,[2] resulting in the appanage of Orkney, Shetland, and the Hebrides to the Norwegian crown for nearly four centuries thereafter. The control may often have been lax, or even interrupted, but the claim of conquest and a certain amount of supremacy were never abandoned until the convention between Magnus IV. of Norway and Alexander III. of Scotland in 1266, as a consequence of King Hakon's ill-fated

---

[1] Henderson's *Iceland*, vol. ii. pp. 80, 81 ; *Celto-Scand.*, p. 21. See *The Saga of King Olaf Tryggwason*, p. 169, where it is also stated that she was buried, in accordance with her own commands, on the seashore below high-water mark.

On the other hand, *Laxdœla Saga, Translated from the Icelandic by Muriel A. C. Press*, 1899 (p. 12), expressly describes the burial of Aud (or *Unn*) with pagan rites, A.D. 920. The same translator (p. 5) dates the emigration of Ketil Flatnef to Scotland as A.D. 890,—in his old age, and after Thorstein the Red, his grandson, had attained manhood ; although it is also stated (*Ibid.*, p. 3) that Ketil gave as his reason for declining a proposal of his sons, Bjorn and Helgi, in favour of Iceland, the preference 'to go west over the sea, . . . for there he had harried far and wide,'—plainly inferring earlier visits to the Sudreys before this final self-exile. Nevertheless, it appears hopeless to reconcile the various chronologies ; as to which, *The Saga Library* (Morris and Magnusson), and Dasent, in *Burnt Njal*, seem to remain the highest authorities so venturesome as to enter much into dates.

[2] *Flateyjarbok*, quoted in *Orkneyinga Saga*, p. 203 ; also *Saga Library*, vol. iii. p. 113. The reasons for assigning this date to King Harald's first expedition are given, *antea*, p. 182.

venture. And even then, by this treaty made at Perth, the Isle of Man and the Sudreys (Orkney and Shetland being specially excepted from the cession) were only given up in consideration of a yearly payment of 100 merks, in perpetuity to the King of Norway or his representatives at Kirkwall Cathedral, within the octave of the nativity of St. John the Baptist.[1]

In regard to religion, many of the Norse settlers in the Sudreys had, during the latter half of the ninth century, accepted Christianity under the influence of Iona.[2] It would seem that the new faith became partially spread among the Northmen in the Hebrides at least a century before its adoption in Norway, pressed there, at the point of the sword, by King Olaf Tryggwason upon most unwilling converts, A.D. 995 to 1000.[3] In Iceland, on 24th June 1000, the Althing proclaimed Christianity as a law of the land, commanding, in addition to belief in the creed of the Trinity, all men to 'leave off idol-worship, not expose children to perish, and not eat horseflesh,' under the penalty of outlawry for open transgression.[4]

---

[1] *Celto-Norman.*, pp. 52-55 ; Munch, p. 132.

[2] St. Columba settled at Iona in A.D. 563.

[3] This Olaf Tryggwason, when upon one of his viking-voyages before becoming king of Norway, had been baptized by the monks of Scilly in A.D. 993, and was thenceforth a zealous propagandist of Christianity. It is to be noted that about the year 986 Iona was ravaged by the Norsemen (*Annals of Ulster*, quoted in *Collectanea*, pp. 266, 267, the invaders being there called *Danes*).

[4] *Burnt Njal*, vol. ii. p. 79. Dasent in *Ibid.*, vol. i. p. xxvi, says that the use of horse-flesh as food was equivalent to eating meat offered to idols—*i.e.* horses sacrificed before heathen altars.

Some fifty years earlier, Hakon the Good,[1] King of Norway, had made strenuous endeavours to establish the Christian faith in his land, though the pagan element remained so strong that the odallers at Drontheim compelled their king to eat some pieces of horse-flesh.[2]   Later, about the year 1020, King Olaf Haraldson[3] followed in the same lines as his predecessor, Olaf Tryggwason, of baptism by force, but was unable to prevent his converts from making 'blood-offerings for peace and a good winter season.'[4]   The *real* Christianising of the people must have been a very slow process, and, without doubt, pagan rites would continue in Norway itself at least far into the eleventh century, and perhaps, incidentally, nearly as long in its more advanced western colony, the Sudreys.   But, as a rule, burnt-burials and the sacrifice or eating of horses,[5] may be regarded as unusual in the Orkneys or Hebrides after about the years 1050 to 1100 at the very latest.

[1] Son of Harald Harfagri, and foster-son of Athelstan, King of England ; reigned *ca.* 935-960.

[2] *Saga Library*, vol. iii. p. 171.

[3] St. Olaf, who reigned 1015-1030 ; *Orkneyinga Saga*, pp. 8 and cxxvi.

[4] *Saga Library*, vol. iv. pp. 193-194.   *Human* sacrifice had formerly been practised among the Northmen.   It is said that about the year 995 Earl Hakon 'the bad' offered up his son Erling immediately before his sea-fight with the Jomsburg vikings (*Ibid.*, vol. iii. p. 283).   These human sacrifices appear, however, to have been rare.

A curious description by an eye-witness early in the tenth century (Ahmed Ibn Fozlan) exists of the cremation of a Norse chief, together with his ship and a *human* victim.   This was on the upper part of the Volga (*Orkneyinga Saga*, pp. cxvii-cxx).

[5] The mere *eating* of horseflesh, being, as we have already seen, a test of paganism as against Christianity.   Burning of the dead body, together with the man's goods, was ordained as a law by Odin, 'but the ashes should men bear out to sea, or bury in the earth ; and over noble men should a mound be raised for the memory of them ; but over all men of any mark should standing stones be raised' (*Saga Library*, vol. iii. p. 20).

In the same way, it may be surmised, that in addition to burnt-burials, those in 'hows'[1] or mounds—the viking with his ship, or horse and armour, or with both together[2]—had been discontinued by about this period. In other words, that in the Sudreys, where such pagan burials or signs of the use of horse-flesh as food are found, these may approximately be assigned to a period previous to the eleventh century.

This is a most difficult point, since in archæology no sharp lines of demarcation are to be found, old practices being often followed long after their normal era. But the earlier vikings had from the ninth century settled in the Sudreys, where the new faith had already been in vogue since the time of St.

[1] According to Dasent, in *Burnt Njal*, vol. i. pp. cxxi-cxxiii, the Norse burials in Iceland were *unburnt*, the body being merely laid in a cairn, with goods and arms, sometimes in a ship, but always in a chamber formed of timber or stone, over which earth and gravel were piled. A last duty of the priest was to bind 'hell-shoon' upon the feet of the dead, in which they should walk in Valhalla. On the other hand, as to 'chambered-cairns,' Dr. Joseph Anderson in *Proc. Soc. Antiq. Scot.* vol. xii. pp. 346, 347, notes that 'the common or typical Norwegian barrow of the viking time was destitute of cist or chamber.'

[2] In the *Story of Egil Skallagrimsson* (London, 1893), p. 124, is recorded the burial in Iceland of Egil's father—a famous smith—under a mound, together with his horse, weapons, and smithy tools. This was in 933. When Egil himself died, *ca.* 983, he was laid with his weapons and raiment in a sepulchral mound (*Ibid.*, pp. 197, 215). Three ship-burials have been discovered at Pierowall in Orkney (*Scotland in Pagan Times— The Iron Age*, pp. 57-59). In 1891 a burnt-burial—including man, ship, and horse—was found in sand-hills at Kiloran, Colonsay (*Proc. Soc. Antiq. Scot.*, vol. xxvi. pp. 61-62). Again, according to the old *Stat. Acc.*, at Cornaig-beg in Tiree have been unearthed skeletons of men and horses, laid with swords and armour. From a grave in Tiree (exact locality unspecified) came also a bronze tortoise-shaped brooch of the viking age, together with a heavy bronze pin (*Proc. Soc. Antiq. Scot.*, vol. x. pp. 554, 555, 560).

The *New Stat. Acc.*, vol. xiv. p. 207, records the discovery of the skeleton of a man (with armour) and a horse in the sand-drift on Watersay, the next island south of Barra. The writer has also been credibly informed of a similar burial in Coll, near Arinabost.

Columba, a period of three hundred years, and it was *from* these western islands that Christianity became widely spread in Norway proper by A.D. 1000. Heathen rites would probably thus cease much sooner in the earlier-taught west than in the home-country itself.

There only remains to notice some of the more definite references to the Sudreys in those of the Sagas of Orkney and Iceland which are readily accessible through translations. Of Ketil Flatnef and his family (*ca.* 852 onwards) sufficient mention for our purpose has already been made.

Before the year 880, Eyvind Eastman (whose daughter Thurida married Thorstein the Red) had his son Helgi the Lean fostered in the Sudreys, but the child's condition (whence his nickname) after two years was so little to the credit of those in charge that Helgi was then removed to Ireland.[1] This incident, coupled with Helgi's after marriage to Thorunna Hyrna (a double bond with the family of Ketil Flatnef), would argue some distinct connection between Eyvind Eastman and the Hebrides. Kol, the companion of Orlyg (who was Ketil's nephew, and had also been fostered in the Sudreys) in his emigration to Iceland about the same period, is evidently identical with the Kol who was a friend of Aud, and married Thorgerda, daughter of Thorstein the Red, settling in Laxardal near Breidafjord in Iceland.[2] This Dala-Kol was the ancester of an important family, and would seem to have

---

[1] *Celto-Scand.*, p. 24.

[2] *Ibid.*, pp. 15, 19, 22. His mother was Vedra-Grimsun, and he was known in Iceland as Dala-Kol (*Ibid.*, pp. 19, 22).

kept up his relations with the Hebrides, as we hear of his grand-daughter Hallgerda (daughter of Hauskuld) having been fostered by a man of the Sudreys, Thiostolf by name,[1] but whether in the western isles or in Iceland is not stated.

During the rule of Sigurd Hlodverson (*Digri*, or 'the Stout') as earl of Orkney, *ca.* 980-1014, there was in the Sudreys a tributary chief, named Earl Gilli, to whom Earl Sigurd sent Kari, son of Solmund, 'to gather scatts.'[2] A few years later, 989-993, this Kari joined the sons of Njal in a viking expedition to Wales and then to the Isle of Man, in the course of which they slew Dungal (or Duncan) a son of Godred, king of Man.[3] On their return voyage towards Iceland, holding north from the Isle of Man, they came to Coll (*Thadan heldu their nordr til Kolu*[4]), there receiving a kindly welcome from Earl Gilli, and remaining some time with him. Thence, accompanied by their friendly host, they went on to the Orkneys, where, next spring, Earl Sigurd of Orkney gave his sister Nereid in marriage to Earl Gilli, who took his bride home with him to the Hebrides, Kari and the sons of Njal sailing to Iceland that summer.[5]

[1] *Burnt Njal*, vol. i. p. 30. Hallgerda seems to have been born about the year 940.

[2] *Ibid.*, vol. ii. p. 11.

[3] According to Munch, p. 44, this was in 989, but the chronology of the *Burnt Njal*, vol. i. p. cciii, and vol. ii. pp. 39, 40, would give the date as 993.

[4] *Rolls*, vol. i. p. 324. Munch, p. 44, identifies Kolu or Koln with the island of Colonsay, but all other authorities agree that it was Coll. Köln is now, as it was in the Saga days (only then without the *diæresis*), also the name of Cologne, upon the Rhine (*The Saga of King Olaf Tryggwason*, pp. 75, 465). *Kol* as a proper name seems to have represented both *Nicholas* and the adjective *black*, the latter being Norse.

[5] *Rolls*, vol. i. p. 324; *Burnt Njal*, vol. ii. pp. 39, 40. Nereid is elsewhere named as Svanlaug or Hvarflod in the Icelandic, and as Gormflaith or Kormlod in a Celtic form (*Rolls*,

At Christmas, 1013, Earl Gilli revisited Orkney upon the invitation of his brother-in-law, Earl Sigurd,[1] and after returning to the Sudreys next spring (the year of the battle of Clontarf) had a dream in which a man came to him from Ireland, and told of the death of King Brian Boroimhe (Boru).[2]

The *Heimskringla* (*Saga Library*, vol. iv. pp. 12-18) gives a somewhat detailed account of the *vestrviking* of Olaf Haraldson, and of his numerous victories. These include the taking of William's-town at Grislo Polla, and Gunnvallds-borg at Seliopolla, localities which one could wish to identify with places in Coll and Tiree which bear very similar names. As, however, the scene of his viking successes may just as probably have been the north-west corner of France, these details are better relegated to a footnote.[3]

vol. i. pp. 326, 420) ; but these seem all to be mere synonyms with *Nereid* or *sea-nymph*. See also the close of this chapter, where it is suggested that Earl Gilli was not improbably a lineal ancestor of the famous Somerled. In connection with the Hill-forts of Coll (No. 14, upon Gallanach farm), *Cnoc Ghillibreidhe* is mentioned as the local name of a neighbouring isolated hillock which has traces of ramparts upon its summit. This may possibly have associations with Earl Gilli or some of his successors.

[1] *Burnt Njal*, vol. ii. p. 322. *Rolls*, vol. i. p. 326.

[2] *Burnt Njal*, vol. ii. p. 342 ; *Rolls*, vol. i. p. 337. Earl Sigurd the Stout also fell at the battle of Clontarf in 1014 ; *Rolls*, vol. i. p. 239.

[3] Olaf Haraldson (Olaf the Thick), afterwards King of Norway and 'Saint Olaf,' had spent 'three winters' helping King Æthelred ii. (the Unready) of England against the Danes. After Æthelred's death in the spring of 1016, Olaf went south across the sea to Ringsfjord (probably in Normandy or Brittany) and took a castle among the hills there, a resort of vikings. The chronicle then runs, ' *Tha hellt Olafr konungr lidi sino vestr til Grislo polla, oc bardiz kar, vid vikinga fyrir Vilhialmsbæ*' (*Celto-Scand.*, p. 96), which we may venture to translate, 'Then took King Olaf his forces west to Grislo polla, and fought there with vikings before William's town.' It would be most interesting to know what was the exact locality of this 'eleventh' battle of Olaf. The word 'vestr' taken in connection

In the years 1093, 1098, and 1102,[1] King Magnus (Barelegs) of Norway made three several expeditions to the western islands, for the purpose of enforcing his rule in these quarters, where it had become very weak.   From the date of his second voyage in 1098 comes the more complete subjugation of Orkney and the Sudreys to the Norwegian throne.   On this occasion King Magnus took prisoners the two Earls of Orkney (Paul and Erlend), and sending them to Norway, left his young son Sigurd (afterwards surnamed *Jorsalafari* or 'Jerusalem-farer') in command of these islands.   Thence he himself proceeded south to Lewis[2] and

with the use of the term 'vestr-viking' as applying peculiarly to piracies in Great Britain and Ireland (*Collectanea*, p. 64), and more especially with the occurrence of the whole phrase a few months later in reference to this very expedition (*Saga Library*, vol. iv. p. 27, A.D. 1016), might lead us to regard *Grislo polla* as somewhere in Ireland or the Sudreys.   There is a Grishipol in Coll, a name which would precisely suit, and near it are the remains of at least two Duns or rude castles, but the argument is admitted to be inconclusive.

Olaf's next (twelfth) battle was west in Fetlafjord, which may designate either the Pentland Firth or the narrows at Fetlar in the Shetlands.   Of the *thirteenth* fight we read (*Celto-Scand.*, p. 96, also *Saga Library*, vol. iv. p. 19), ' *Thadan for Olafr konungr allt sudr til Seliopolla, atti thar orrosto ; thar vann hann borg tha er heiter Gunnvaldsborg ; hun var mikil oc forn, oc thar tok han Jarl, er fyrir red borginni, er het Geirsidr,*'—' Thence fared King Olaf south to Seliopolla, and there gave battle ; there was a town (or castle) large and old, known as Gunnvalldsborg, and he took prisoner the jarl, named Geirsid, who had ruled the town.'   This place, Seliopolla, one could equally wish to identify with Heylipol in Tiree, not far from which, lying halfway between Tiree and Coll, is an island named Gunna, where still remain old fortifications.   It is only fair to add that after this victory ' King Olaf went with his host west to Charles-water' (? the Bay of Biscay) with the purpose of pressing on through the Straits of Gibraltar (Norfi-sound) into 'Jerusalem-world,' but, in consequence of a dream, changed his plans and returned to the north (*Saga Library*, vol. iv. p. 20).   King Olaf Haraldson died in 1030.

[1] Munch, pp. 54-58, and *Orkneyinga Saga*, p. xxxiv.

[2] *Ljodhus* in the Icelandic ; *Rolls*, vol. i. p. 69, etc.   It seems probable that the name Lewis is derived from Earl Hlodver (great-grandson of Thorstein the Red, on the maternal side), the father of Sigurd the Stout, and grandfather of Thorfinn (*Rolls*, vol. i. pp. xliii, and liii) ;

Uist,[1] harrying both there and in Skidi (Skye) and Tyrvist, which
is the Saga form for Tiree. It is said that Donald Bane, then
ruling in Scotland, agreed with King Magnus that all the western
islands, 'between which and the mainland he could pass in a vessel
with the rudder shipped,' should belong to Norway. 'Thereupon
King Magnus landed in Satiri (Kintyre) and had a boat drawn
across the isthmus,' and thus gained the whole of Kintyre south
of Tarbert. That year King Magnus wintered in the Sudreys.[2] In
1103, Olaf Bitling,[3] son of Godred Crowan,[4] king of Man, became
tributary ruler over the Sudreys (doubtless under the Norwegian
King Sigurd *Jorsalafari*, son of Magnus Barelegs),[5] and continued
his comparatively peaceful reign for the space of fifty years, one of
his daughters marrying the famous Somerled of Argyll.[6]

Munch, p. 43, and *Rolls*, vol. iii. p. 445, both treat *Hlodver* as synonymous with Lewis, although
the first-named authority elsewhere states (p. xix) that 'Lewis is only an alteration of the
Norwegian *Ljodhus* (the 'sounding-house').' Hlodver was Earl of Orkney, and probably
ruled the Sudreys also. He died *ca.* 980, and was succeeded by his son Sigurd, who
(according to Munch, p. 45) long held these islands ; while Thorfinn is distinctly stated to
have possessed the whole of the Hebrides, and to have been earl for at least fifty years till his
death in 1064 (*Orkneyinga Saga*, pp. 31 and 44).

[1] 'Vist' in the Saga (*Celto-Scand.*, pp. 231 and 232). Munch, p. xix, says that North
Uist, Harris, and South Uist were called *Ivist* which means simply 'dwelling' or 'habitation.'
We would rather incline to the derivation from 'west' or its analogue.

[2] 1098-1099, *Orkneyinga Saga*, p. 56, and *Rolls*, vol. i. pp. 71-72.

[3] Bitling='little bit' or 'the tiny,' probably in allusion to Olaf's stature. His second
wife was Ingibiorg, daughter of Hakon, Earl of Orkney (Munch, p. 7 ; *Orkneyinga Saga*,
p. cxxxiii ; and *Rolls*, vol. i. p. 82).

[4] And grandson of Harald the Black of 'Iceland' (Ysland) or more probably of *Islay* (Yle)
where Godred Crowan died (Munch, pp. 3, 4, and 51).

[5] King Magnus Barelegs was killed in Ireland, 1103.

[6] Munch, pp. 7, 9, 73, 78. Olaf Bitling seems also to have been known as 'Olaf the
Red,' *Collectanea*, p. 283. The authority cited, 'a fragment of a manuscript history of the

Contemporary with Olaf Bitling was Earl Rognvald II. of Orkney (originally named Kali Kol's son), born *ca.* 1100, and joint earl from *ca.* 1129 till his death in 1159.[1] His grandfather was Kali Sæbjornarson (*i.e.* son of Sea-bear), a man of Agdir in Norway and a great friend of King Magnus Barelegs, whom he had accompanied in his western expedition of 1098, during the winter of which year Kali, son of Sea-bear, died of his wounds in the Sudreys, leaving a son Kol. To Kol, Kali's son, by way of compensation for the loss of his father, King Magnus next year gave in marriage Gunnhild, daughter of Earl Erlend and sister to St. Magnus, of which union was born Kali,[2] afterwards re-named Rognvald when he had received from King Sigurd 'Jorsalafari' half of the Orkney earldom.[3] It was by his father Kol's advice that Earl Rognvald-Kali in 1137 vowed to his uncle St. Magnus (who had been killed in 1116) that if through the saint's help he should succeed in establishing himself in his half of the earldom, he would build at Kirkwall a magnificent church in his honour.[4] This was the origin of the famous cathedral

---

Macdonalds,' states that Olaf the Red was king of Man, Islay, Mull, and the islands south of Ardnamurchan, while Godfrey (or perhaps rather *Godred*) the Black had possession of the isles to the north of that point. Somerled's marriage with Olaf's daughter is also mentioned in the same connection (*Collectanea*, pp. 282, 288).

[1] *Rolls*, vol. iii. p. 215. He was killed on the 20th of August 1159. According to *Ibid.*, vol. i. pp. xiv and 197-199, the story of Earl Rognvald is to be taken as almost strictly historical; it even gives exact dates, such as the above, one of which—the slaying of Erlend on 21st December 1154, 'four nights before Yule' and 'at full moon'—has been astronomically verified.

[2] *Rolls*, vol. i. pp. 68-73.   [3] *Ibid.*, p. 103.   [4] *Ibid.*, p. 119.

of St. Magnus, commenced within the year, and of which the plan and erection were under the charge of Rognvald's father Kol.[1]

At Christmas in the year 1135 or 1136, Swein Asleifson (already mentioned as an active viking of the island of Gairsay) had slain his namesake Swein Briostreip (Breast-rope) at Orphir in Orkney in a drinking quarrel. Bishop William kept Swein Asleifson in Egilsey during Yuletide, and then sent him to Tiree (Tyrvist) to a man named Holdbodi, who was a great chief there.[2] The two became fast friends, and a few years later, after Swein's return to the Orkneys he again visited the Sudreys at the request of Holdbodi, who had been chased out of his home in Tiree by a freebooter from Wales. Swein did not find Holdbodi until he had reached the Isle of Man, when both of them went out with five ships and plundered in Wales and on the coast of Ireland. In the course of their viking-voyages, Holdbodi, much to Swein's anger, played his comrade false by making a secret alliance with their chief enemy who occupied a good stronghold in Lundy Island; and it is recorded

---

[1] *Rolls*, vol. i. p. 132. Kol seems to have lived chiefly in Norway, but his son Kali about the year 1116 went thence with some merchants to England (Grimsby), where he met a great company of men both from Norway, Orkney, Scotland, and the Sudreys. There he made friends with Gillikrist, son of King Magnus Barelegs, and afterwards King Harald Gilli of Norway (*Ibid.*, pp. 95 and 104). Earl Rognvald-Kali made a pilgrimage to Jerusalem in 1151-1153, not without some viking-work on the way thither, although he returned by land from Italy (*Ibid.*, pp. 159-179).

[2] *Orkneyinga Saga*, pp. 92-95; *Rolls*, vol. i. pp. 113-116. Holdbodi was the son of Hundi. 'Holdr' seems to stand for a 'freeman' or owner of 'odal' lands.

that Holdbodi never dared to return to the Sudreys.   This was
in 1139-1148.[1]

The first Somerled of Argyll seems to have been born about
the year 1020, 'son of Gilbrigid, King of Innsie Gall,' dying in
1083.[2]   But the celebrated Somerled of the Isles (surnamed
'Hold,' and described as 'regulus Herergaidel'),[3] unquestioned
ancestor of the powerful MacDonalds of the Isles, did not flourish
until the next century.   His parentage is given as the son of
Gil-bride, the son of Gil-adomnan,[4] and Munch argues that the
earlier Somerled (son of Gilbrigid) was *father* of Gil-adomnan,
and further that he (including as a consequence Somerled Hold)
was descended from the Earl Gilli of Coll, who had married a
sister of Sigurd the Stout, Earl of Orkney, about the year
990-994.[5]

Somerled Hold married Ragnhild, daughter of Olaf Bitling,[6]

---

[1] *Orkneyinga Saga*, pp. 116-121 ; *Rolls*, vol. i. pp. 136-141.

[2] Munch, pp. 74 and 75, quoting the *Annals of the Four Masters*. 'Innsie Gall' was
the Irish name for the Sudreys.   Munch, p. 42, considers Somerled to be originally merely
another Norwegian form of 'Vik-ing,' viz. *Sumar-lidi*, or 'summer-wanderer,' and instances
as a parallel case the term 'vetrlidi,' designating a bear gone to take his winter sleep.   A
still earlier Sumarlidi, Earl of Orkney, and son of Earl Sigurd the Stout, died *ca.* 1015
(*Orkneyinga Saga*, p. cxxxii).

[3] Munch, p. 7.

[4] *Celto-Scand.*, p. 294 ; and *Collectanea*, p. 282, 'son of *Gilbert*.'

[5] Munch, pp. 74 and 75.   By this argument, which seems not without good grounds, the
dates would agree with Earl Gilli as being the father of Gilbrigid, king of the Sudreys.
For Earl Gilli, see *antea*.   Munch points out (p. 44) that Gilli is evidently only half of the
name of the Sudreyan earl, 'Gille' meaning 'servant' and being ordinarily prefixed to the
name of some saint, as Gil-brigid, Gil-adomnan, Gil-colum, etc.

[6] See *antea*.

king of Man and the Isles, and had four sons, Dugald, Rognvald
(Reginald), Angus, and Olaf.[1] In his time he had many battles,—
including a sea-fight in 1156 with his brother-in-law Godred,
king of Man, which resulted in a division of the Sudreys,[2]—and
was ultimately killed, with Gille-colum his son,[3] at the battle of
Renfrew in 1164. Others of the name of Somerled are mentioned : one of them, a grandson of Somerled Hold, ruled in the
mainland of Argyll, but was deprived in 1221 by Alexander II.
of Scotland.[4] Olaf the Black, son of Godred, king of Man, and
grandson of Olaf Bitling, held part of the Hebrides until his
death in 1237.[5] From this date it is an easy transition to the
battle of Largs in October 1263, when, as we have already
seen, the Norwegian supremacy in the Sudreys was finally
broken.

Many petty kings or earls of the Isles are named in the Sagas,
but the title cannot be taken as necessarily implying any general
control. It seems indeed that each of the larger islands had

[1] Munch, p. 7, and *Orkneyinga Saga*, p. 181. This marriage, evidently a second one,
may very approximately be placed as *ca.* 1140-1150. Somerled Hold made his home at
Dalir (or ‘the Dales’), somewhere on the west coast of Scotland (*Orkneyinga Saga*, pp. 176,
181, and *Rolls*, vol. i. p. 210). It is through this Reginald or Rognvald that the MacDonalds
of the Isles have their descent, and the Somerled blood, although no doubt with a Norse
intermixture, seems to have been mainly Celtic (see *Collectanea*, p. 285).

[2] Munch, p. 10.

[3] Munch says, ‘his eldest son, Gillecolum’ (p. 94).

[4] Munch, p. 95.

[5] *Ibid.*, pp. 16 and 20. Rognvald, a great warrior, and elder brother of Olaf the Black,
was king of Man, and died in 1229. His son, Godred the Black, succeeded him for one
year (*Rolls*, vol. ii. p. 462 ; Munch, p. 190).

its tributary 'earl' or governor under the Norwegian crown,[1] as in the case of Earl Gilli of Coll.

[1] Munch, p. 83. Rognvald and his father Godred, up to the year 1210, had for a long time paid no 'scatt' to the kings of Norway (*Rolls*, vol. i. p. 233). After the death in 1187 of Godred, king of Man, there were two Reginalds (cousins, both of them grandsons of Olaf Bitling and each styled 'King of the Isles') reigning in the divided Sudreys—one (eldest son of Godred) in the northern or Norwegian division (including Skye, the Long Island, Tiree and Coll, as also Arran), and the other (second son of Somerled) in the southern or Celtic portion. The first-named was treacherously slain in 1229, and appears to have had his chief residence in the island of Coll, being indeed addressed in an Irish poem as 'King of Coll' (Skene's *Celtic Scotland*, vol. iii. pp. 35, 36, 401, 421).

INDEX